FEARGUS O'CONNOR

Irishman and Chartist

Feargus O'Connor : M.P. for County Cork 1832-35

FEARGUS O'CONNOR

Irishman and Chartist

DONALD READ

Lecturer in Modern History, University of Leeds

and

ERIC GLASGOW

LONDON

EDWARD ARNOLD (PUBLISHERS) LTD.

© *Donald Read and Eric Glasgow 1961*

First published 1961

PRINTED IN GREAT BRITAIN
BY CHARLES BIRCHALL & SONS, LTD.,
LIVERPOOL AND LONDON

PREFACE

DURING the last forty years historians have given us a much fuller picture of the course and character of the Chartist movement, the first sustained working-class political agitation in British history. But no biography has yet appeared of Feargus O'Connor, the colourful Irish demagogue who made himself the leader of the Chartists. As G. D. H. Cole once remarked, O'Connor has long stood out as by far the most influential figure in nineteenth-century British history still without a biography. The present book is the first to tell the story of his career. As well as using the familiar sources for Chartist history —including O'Connor's own *Northern Star*, the first great British popular newspaper—it draws upon previously little-used sources in Ireland. From these it traces the early career of O'Connor as an agitator in agricultural Ireland, linking this up with his later activity as an agitator in the new England of the Industrial Revolution. O'Connor *became* a Chartist: he was always an Irishman. "O'Connor is an Irishman in the strictest sense of the word." remarked the *Nottingham Mercury* even after he had been for nearly ten years the Chartist leader in England; "Irish in all his thoughts" (Oct. 1, 1847). This is the theme which underlies the biography.

A word needs to be said about the division of labour between the two authors. Dr. Glasgow has been responsible for research into O'Connor's Irish background and career: Mr. Read has been chiefly responsible for research into his Chartist period and for the actual writing of the book.

Both authors gladly acknowledge assistance from many individuals and institutions both in England and in Ireland. In particular, they wish to thank Asa Briggs, W. H. Chaloner, H. L. Conner, Miss D. O'Neill Daunt, Mrs. I Davidson, N. Harding, A. J. Hawkes, Miss R. O'Higgins; and the staffs of the public reference libraries of Leeds, Manchester, Nottingham and Birmingham, of the Public Record Office, the British Museum, the National Library of Ireland, and the library of the King's Inns, Dublin, of the Castle Museum, York, and of the University Libraries of Leeds and Manchester.

CONTENTS

CHAPTER I

FAMILY BACKGROUND

WE begin on a note of uncertainty. Feargus O'Connor claimed,
and was constantly to repeat to humble Chartist audiences, that
his family was descended from Roderick O'Connor, high king of
Ireland in the eleventh century. In fact, the evidence for this is
confused and uncertain. Briefly, the royal tradition stated that
the family of Feargus O'Connor came from the supposedly royal
Kerry line of the O'Connor clan. Two different stories sought
to explain how Feargus's branch of the family reached Co. Cork,
where it was certainly established by the beginning of the eighteenth century. According to one version, a Kerry O'Connor
ancestor of Feargus was murdered by Cromwellian soldiers near
Tralee in 1652. His widow fled across the mountains to Bandon
in Co. Cork, and took her infant son, Cornelius, with her. She
remained undiscovered, and having quilted a store of gold coins
in her cloak, was able to live in Bandon comfortably. To make her
disguise more effective she changed her name to the English-
sounding "Conner" and brought up Cornelius (d. 1712) as a
Protestant. He became a prosperous merchant in Bandon and
acquired some property.[1]

The alternative version of the story gave Cornelius Conner a
different background, describing him not as a Catholic Irish
refugee but as a Protestant English merchant. John O'Connell,
son of the Irish "Liberator" with whom Feargus O'Connor
quarrelled violently in the mid-1830s, referred scoffingly to
Cornelius Conner in his memoirs, thinking that he had thereby

---

1. Sir J. B. Burke, *A Second Series of Vicissitudes of Families*
   (1860), article on the O'Connors of Connerville, based upon
   information supplied by W. J. O'Neill Daunt (*A Life Spent
   for Ireland* (1896), 160).

entirely discredited Feargus's claim to Irish royal ancestry.[2] But, in fact, this version, while admitting the English connections of Cornelius Conner, still claimed him as a descendant of the ancient kings of Ireland. Philip Kerry, the story ran, an Elizabethan ancestor of Cornelius Conner, merchant, was a relative of John O'Connor Kerry, head of the clan.[3]

We cannot be sure how much or how little of this contradictory traditional history of the family of Feargus O'Connor is true. But from Cornelius the descent is clear. His son Daniel greatly extended the family possessions, mainly as a result of the confiscations which followed the revolution of 1688 in Ireland. The Conners became prominent citizens of Bandon. Daniel had a large family, but outstanding among his children was the second son, William, who represented Bandon in the Irish parliament from 1761 until his death in 1766. William Conner added further to the family heritage by building Connerville on his property west of Bandon. In its final form Connerville resembled more a village than a single house, the servants occupying a cluster of neighbouring cottages.

William was followed in possession of Connerville by his son Roger Conner. In 1753 Roger made a socially advantageous marriage into the Longfield family, which had its seat near Mallow. He died in 1798, two years before his wife's brother was created Viscount Longueville as a bribe for supporting the Act of Union with England.

The sons of Roger Conner, father and uncles of Feargus O'Connor, were a lively set. The story of the royal descent of the family now became prominent, at a time of reviving national feeling. Roger Conner may have fabricated the whole thing to assist the social and political advancement of his family. Be this as it may, his sons believed in their descent from Roderick O'Connor and showed a royal tendency to stop at nothing. The eldest son Daniel (1754-1846) eloped to Bristol. To pay the damages awarded against him he had to sell his interest in the family property to his younger brother Roger (1763-1834), the

---

2. J. O'Connell, *Recollections and Experiences during a Parliamentary Career* (1849), I, 90-91.

3. R. R. Madden, *The United Irishmen* (1857-60), second series, second ed., II, 228-29.

fourth son, father of Feargus, for £5,000. Daniel's eldest son, another Daniel, eventually returned to Ireland, claimed the western portion of the estate and in 1824 built Manch House upon it. From him is descended the one branch of the family which still retains part of the ancestral property.

Other sons of Roger Conner were Robert, the third son, and Arthur (1763-1852), the fifth and youngest. Arthur, Robert and Roger, the father of Feargus O'Connor, all became deeply involved in Irish politics during the disturbed last decade of the eighteenth century. Characteristically, they all flew to extremes, Arthur and Roger changing their surname to "O'Connor" and becoming United Irishmen (though they remained Protestants), Robert becoming a fervent loyalist.

Arthur O'Connor was one of the most active of the United Irishmen.[4] He sought to set up an Irish republic on the French Revolutionary model and visited Europe to interview the French general Hoche about his plans for the invasion of Ireland in 1796. In 1798 he was tried for treason. He was acquitted but subsequently imprisoned at Fort George, near Inverness, on another charge. He was not released until after the Peace of Amiens in 1802 and was then required to go into exile in France. Napoleon made him a general, and he married a daughter of the philosopher Condorcet. He bought an estate near Nemours, once belonging to Mirabeau, but took only a slight part in French politics, publishing a few pamphlets. In 1834 he was allowed to pay a hurried visit to Co. Cork to dispose of his Irish property, which had been badly embezzled by his brother Roger. J. A. Froude castigated him as having "the polish of cultivation externally [but] with the inner nature of a savage".[5] This was unfair, for Arthur O'Connor was certainly a sincere and quite able idealist. He proved his sincerity by sacrificing the prospect of a large legacy (said by Feargus to be nearly £20,000)[6] promised him by his loyalist uncle Lord Longueville, and also the seat in the Irish parliament which his uncle, a considerable borough proprietor, had given him. In his

---

4. Madden, *United Irishmen*, II, 228-358; *D.N.B.*
5. J. A. Froude, *The English in Ireland in the Eighteenth Century* (1872-74), III, 321.
6. *A Series of Letters from Feargus O'Connor, Esq. Barrister-at-Law to Daniel O'Connell, Esq. M.P.* (1836), 30.

native district Arthur O'Connor is today talked of with greater readiness and pride than his nephew Feargus. Arthur's high reputation as a patriot helped to make that of Feargus in the next generation. Thomas Cooper, the Leicester Chartist, thought that not half a dozen Chartists "cared a fig" about the boasted royal descent of the O'Connors; "but the connection of his family with the "United Irishmen" and patriotic sufferers of the last century, rendered him a natural representative of the cause of political liberty".[7]

Arthur O'Connor's brother, Robert, had equally emphatic views, but on the loyalist side, and he sought strenuously to get his brothers hanged for treason. He formed a corps of yeomanry in Co. Cork and with characteristic egocentricity boasted that he would invade France, capture Napoleon and exhibit him in a cage at Fort Robert, the mansion which he had built for himself on the western part of the estate.[8]

Roger O'Connor, the father of Feargus, shared the revolutionary opinions of his brother Arthur; but while his brother was a republican, Roger seems to have wanted to set up an Irish monarchy with himself (as descended from Roderick O'Connor) as king.[9] He was educated at Trinity College, Dublin, and called to the bar, although he never practised seriously. He began as a loyalist, joining the Muskerry yeomanry and helping to suppress Whiteboy outbreaks. But under the influence of the French Revolution he passed over to the patriotic side. In the years before the outbreak of 1798 he was a leader of the United Irishmen in Co. Cork, playing a double game, outwardly loyal but really disaffected. Connerville was a good centre for intrigue, rather isolated yet near the coast where a French landing might be expected. Roger hospitably entertained the soldiers sent to meet Hoche's expedition of 1796, but all the time he was organising the peasants in patriotic unions. Although himself a Protestant, he worked closely with the Roman Catholic parish clergy, who had great influence over the people. Eventually he came under sus-

---

7. *The Life of Thomas Cooper,* by Himself (2nd ed., 1872), 180.
8. Burke, *Vicissitudes of Families,* 33-35.
9. Cobbett's *Political Register,* May 12, 1810; Madden, *United Irishmen,* III, 590-612; *D.N.B.*; M. W. Patterson, *Sir Francis Burdett and his Times* (1931), ch. VII.

picion. His house was searched, but he was able to escape to England. On his return to Ireland, however, he was captured and imprisoned in Cork. While in prison, like his son Feargus when he was imprisoned for Chartism, Roger O'Connor sought to acquire a halo of martyrdom. A flattering catalogue of his virtues, with a portrait, appeared in *Walker's Hibernian Magazine* for March 1798, almost certainly written by himself. Roger was subsequently imprisoned with his brother Arthur at Fort George. He was released in 1801 but not allowed to live in Ireland. He therefore settled near London, where Feargus received his earliest education. In 1803 he was allowed to return to Ireland, but not to Co. Cork. In consequence he disposed of Connerville on long lease and bought for £40,000 (never fully paid) the large estate of Dangan in Co. Meath. This was a great mistake. It alienated, for good as it turned out, the oldest part of the family property, and saddled the family with much heavier financial responsibilities than it could support. Roger's ideas of his social standing were beyond his means. He said that he wanted Dangan as a suitable residence in which to entertain Napoleon when the French had occupied Ireland. His ambitions with respect to Napoleon thus vied with those of his brother Robert on the loyalist side.

The expense of keeping up Dangan led Roger O'Connor into two discreditable episodes. First a fire broke out at the house soon after he had insured it for £5,000; and then in 1812 the Galway mail-coach was robbed. At the time, Roger's culpability could not be proved in either incident, and he was acquitted when he faced the delayed charge of mail-coach robbery in 1817. But in later years he liked to hint at his bravado in carrying out such a coup, although he claimed that his motive was not vulgar gain but the possession of incriminating love-letters which had passed between Sir Francis Burdett, the English Radical, and Lady Oxford. He claimed that these letters were being sent by the mail to an eminent King's Counsel. Feargus O'Connor and his brothers probably assisted their father in the escapade.

Few men would rob a mail-coach, either for money or to save the reputation of a friend. Roger O'Connor was clearly unbalanced, probably by the end of his life positively insane, and his son Feargus was to go the same way. Yet Roger, like Feargus after him, had much personal charm and had gifts as a wit and writer. Some of his writings were indeed superior to those of Feargus for sheer vivacity and imagination; their defect (a defect passed on to his son) was that there was often no clear line drawn between fact and fiction. His most substantial work, the *Chronicles of Eri*, published in 1822, was also his most fantastic, purporting to prove by means of documents that the pagan civilisation of Ireland had been ruined by the advent of Christianity. All the documents produced by O'Connor were probably products of his own fertile imagination.

Soon after his trial in 1817 Roger O'Connor probably left Dangan, and for the rest of his life he seems to have wandered a good deal, finishing in a cottage at Ballincollig, Co. Cork, with a peasant girl whom he called his 'Princess of Kerry'. To the end he stuck tenaciously to his royal aspirations. His portrait with his hand upon the Irish crown formed the frontispiece to the *Chronicles of Eri*. He habitually signed himself simply 'O'Connor', in analogy with the peerage. When he died in 1834 he was buried at his own wish in the ancestral tomb of the MacCarthys at Kilcrea, Co. Cork. They were the ancient lords of Munster, long since dispossessed by the English, and O'Connor evidently held them in honour.

Roger O'Connor married twice. By his first wife, Louisa Anna Strahan, whom he married in 1784 and who died in 1787, he had a son, who subsequently emigrated to Tasmania, and a daughter. His second wife was Wilhelmina Bowen, of the celebrated Bowenscourt in Co. Cork, whom he married in 1788 and who died in 1808. His children by her were Arthur (d. 1828); Francis Burdett, who went out to South America in 1819 to serve under Bolivar and did well there; Roger; Feargus Edward, the Chartist leader; Mary, Harriet and Wilhelmina.

The history of the family of Feargus O'Connor is thus rather complicated, but it is vital to bear it in mind when studying his career. His family was Irish, revolutionary and believed itself to be royal. O'Connor's life-story was much influenced by this background.

CHAPTER II

EARLY YEARS

THE date of birth of Feargus O'Connor is not easily decided. The baptismal registers for the parish of Kinneigh at the end of the eighteenth century, the parish in which Connerville stood, were among the many destroyed in the Four Courts at Dublin during the civil strife of 1922. The generally accepted date, given for example by Graham Wallas in his article in the *Dictionary of National Biography*, has been July 18, 1794. Wallas accepted the statement made in 1855 by T. M. Wheeler in his memoir of O'Connor prefaced to the printed version of the funeral oration delivered by William Jones. But O'Neill Daunt, cousin and neighbour of O'Connor, in his memoirs, and both *The Times* and the *Annual Register* in their obituaries, gave 1796 as O'Connor's birth-year.[1] Yet a third year was suggested by O'Connor's application in 1830 to be admitted a barrister; he claimed that he was thirty years old on July 18, 1829.[2] This confirms the day and month generally accepted but confuses the question of the year still further. O'Connor, however, probably shared Cobbett's tendency to call himself younger than he was, especially as he wasted several years in young manhood before settling down to his legal training. 1799 would make him very young when he first went to school between 1801 and 1803; but if he were born in 1796 he would be a suitable age, five or six, to start school between these dates. Further evidence supports the year 1796 rather than either 1799 or 1794. In a letter dated January 30, 1815 (part of which

1. W. J. O'Neill Daunt, *Eighty-Five Years of Irish History 1800-1885* (1886), I, 228; *The Times*, Sept. 3, 1855; *Annual Register, 1855*, Appendix to Chronicle, 302; *Gentleman's Magazine*, XLIV, new series (1855), 545.
2. Records of the King's Inns, Dublin.

is quoted later in this chapter) O'Connor's father remonstrated against the intention of Feargus to marry, reminding him that he was not of age. If Feargus had been born in 1794 and was only six months short of his twenty-first birthday this point would not have carried much weight at this date; but if he were two-and-a-half years short of twenty-one it might. If, on the other hand, Feargus had been born in 1799 he would have been only fifteen-and-a-half at this time when he was aspiring to marry. This seems conclusive against 1799 as his real year of birth. At the date of his father's letter Feargus was still at school but was excused from the usual routine of the classroom because of his mature age for a schoolboy.[3] He would hardly have been at school at all if aged twenty-and-a-half : eighteen-and-a-half would seem a more likely age. It seems reasonable to conclude, therefore, that Feargus O'Connor was born not in 1794 or in 1799 but on July 18, 1796.

1796 was the year of the threatened French invasion of Ireland under Hoche, of which both his father and his uncle had great hopes. Feargus was thus born, probably at Connerville, into an unsettled family atmosphere. This atmosphere was to continue throughout his childhood and adolescence. His father was carried away to prison soon after his birth, and during infancy Feargus was left with his mother. Our main source for the story of his schooldays is his own account given in the *National Instructor* in 1850. Unfortunately it is not easy to disentangle fact from fiction in his narrative. His first school, however, was apparently at Streatham, near London, kept by a Mr. Finlay, 'a fine, noble, independent fellow and a great admirer of my father'.[4] Feargus probably started there about 1801 after Roger O'Connor had been released from Fort George and came to live near London. Feargus, as we can well imagine, was not a very submissive pupil and seems to have progressed more in boxing than in knowledge. His next school was apparently at Clonmel in Tipperary, probably in 1803 when his father was allowed to go back to Ireland. Feargus next entered Dr. Leney's school near Dublin, where he managed to stay for eight years, performing numerous pranks. Some of these were far beyond the usual range of boyish escapades, and he was finally expelled. Feargus's application for admission to the King's

3. *National Instructor* (1850), 24.
4. Ibid, 23.

Inns in 1819 mentioned another school near Dublin—that of Dr. Barry at Blackrock—and he may be presumed to have attended this also, perhaps after Dr. Leney had tired of him.

Feargus acquired at school only a thin veneer of culture; but characteristically, his pretensions to knowledge in later life often outran the reality. Thus of the six Latin quotations in his first political pamphlet, published in 1822, Graham Wallas tells us that five contain serious blunders.[5] His veneer of education was sufficient, however, to impress some of the Chartist working-men, like the self-educated Thomas Cooper, who believed that Feargus 'had had the education of a gentleman, and had not lost his relish for Virgil and Horace'.[6]

Whatever schools he may have attended near Dublin, O'Connor did not finish his schooldays there. Although really beyond school-age he went finally to Mr. Willis's establishment at Portarlington, where the diarist J. W. Croker had been a pupil. Being too old for class-teaching, he did very little work but spent much of his time out-of-doors, indulging a passion for horses and riding. This leisurely period was brought to an abrupt end by the discovery that Feargus was conducting a love-affair with one of the daughters of his schoolmaster.[7] For this he was once more expelled from school. The characteristically verbose letter of expostulation, dated January 30, 1815, sent to him by his father is the earliest original record connected with Feargus which we have. It is preserved in the Conner papers at Manch House.

I am made acquainted by Mr. Willis's letter, that you have fancied to fall in love, as it is called, with one of his daughters, and I hear from other quarters that you speak of what is termed 'marrying' her. This is a step more easily taken than retraced ... Have you ever bestowed a thought upon all the horrors attendant upon such an act? ... From what quarter do you expect any means to support yourself, and to answer all the calls which such an encumbrance demands?

Have you thought of my condition, and that of all your brothers and sisters? Who clinging to me in fidelity, as I have

---

5. *D.N.B.*
6. Cooper, *Life*, 273.
7. *National Instructor*, 25-26.

done to them, labour in obscurity without society, with barely the necessaries of life, to keep our rank, till such time as by our unwearied perseverance, we shall be able to live in some manner suitable to our pretensions ... If such is your nature that you could prefer the gratification of your own depraved, debased passion ... never shall you see my face, nor ever during your existence shall you receive, nor any human being proceeding from you, the means of one hour's life from me, nor through me.

... Restore yourself to the bosom of your family ... many months cannot pass till I shall have the means of enabling you to prosecute useful study in the great world, where I have been fondly thinking you will add lustre to your name, not tarnish it; and on this I do rely.

I am, my dear Feargus,

Your tenderly affectionate father and true friend,

O'CONNOR

This letter suggests the straitened circumstances into which the unwise purchase of Dangan had led the family. It also shows the intense family pride of Roger O'Connor. He was deeply disturbed at the prospect of the family dignity being injured by an alliance with the daughter of a mere schoolmaster. He was an advocate of advanced political opinions and yet incongruously he was very conscious of social differences. Feargus himself, as leader of the Chartist masses, never let them forget his high birth.

Feargus was so desperately attached to the girl that for a time he surreptitiously visited her.[8] But eventually love cooled and he accepted his father's advice and gave up thoughts of marriage. He may now have proceeded to Trinity College, Dublin, where his father and uncle Arthur had gone in their time. The last paragraph of his father's letter may have meant that Roger O'Connor intended to send him there. Certainly, it is often stated that Feargus went to Trinity; but the college registers do not contain any name at all resembling that of Feargus Edward O'Connor. The question must therefore be left open.[9]

---

8. *National Instructor*, 26.
9. C. G. D. Burtchaell & T. U. Sadleir (eds.), *Alumni Dublinenses* (new ed., 1935).

The marriage episode was settled, but Feargus was soon engaged in another escapade. Some time between 1815 and 1817 he and his brother Frank, becoming tired of life at Dangan, decided to run away to England in hopes of earning enough money there to set themselves up on a farm. They galloped away on two horses, sold them at Rathcoole and then sailed from Dublin. They landed at Holyhead and walked first to Bath and then to Marlborough in Wiltshire, where they spent six days hay-making. Their money now began to run short, and they decided to go to London to see Sir Francis Burdett, their father's Radical friend, to ask his advice about emigration or to see if he would place them upon a farm. Burdett had already been warned to look out for them and offered them only their fare back to Ireland. Back they went, therefore, to Bristol where they embarked upon a ship bound for Ireland. The vessel almost sank during a storm which left her drifting for a week. At last she was towed into Cork, and the pair returned to Dangan to face their father, who accused them of disgracing the ancient name of their family.[10]

As well as Burdett, most of the other leading English Radicals of the day were known to Roger O'Connor. Significantly for the future, Feargus was brought up in touch with English as well as with Irish Radicalism. The English Radical press was read attentively at Dangan. Feargus remarked in later life that his father required his four sons to read the various Radical writers to him. One son read Cobbett's *Political Register*; another read Leigh Hunt's *Examiner*; a third went through the daily newspapers; while Feargus himself went through Hansard and read out the speeches of the reformers.[11]

Burdett seems to have taken a liking to young Feargus, for when in 1817 he came over to Ireland to help Roger O'Connor at his trial for the mail-coach robbery, he gave Feargus the money he had wanted to stock a farm of his own. But Feargus had now given up the idea of a farm and spent the money instead upon the purchase of horses. If his own story be true, he had some success as a racing man, acquiring a large stable and a staff of grooms. But he lost the lot through backing a bill for a friend. When he became

---

10. *National Instructor*, 40-42.
11. *Northern Star*, July 11, 1846.

member of parliament for Co. Cork he again bought a stud.[12]

The loss of his stud was a less crushing blow to O'Connor than
it might have been because soon afterwards, about 1820, his uncle
Robert died and unexpectedly left him a fortune and the mansion
of Fort Robert. Feargus, with his brothers Roger and Arthur, now
went back to the estate of their ancestors in Co. Cork.[13] The three
daughters of Robert Conner continued to live at Fort Robert,
eligible young ladies who like many female members of the family
combined vivacity with grace. The inevitable happened. Roger
O'Connor married his cousin Elizabeth and Arthur O'Connor
his cousin Mary. Only Feargus avoided matrimony; but he used
his winning manner to persuade the eldest daughter, Anne, to
bequeath him her share of the property. In this fortunate fashion,
therefore, Feargus O'Connor, fourth son of an increasingly im-
poverished family, became a landed proprietor and the possessor
of some means. Without Fort Robert to give him standing Feargus
would never have become member of parliament for Co. Cork
and might never have led the Chartist movement.

Fort Robert stood deep in the country, above the River Bandon,
surrounded by thickly-wooded hills. The approach by road on
horseback was laborious. But though its location was remote, the
site and size of Fort Robert were striking. It stood out prominently
at the top of a slope, its rooms were large, its views of the river and
woods magnificent. This slightly ostentatious residence suited
O'Connor's temperament well. His first years at Fort Robert were
perhaps the happiest of his life. He seems to have taken a real
interest in running the estate. O'Neil Daunt, his neighbour across
the river at Kilcascan, noted in his journals that one of O'Connor's
most pleasing characteristics was his care for the welfare of his
labourers, whom he paid well and promptly. O'Connor reduced
the price of potatoes for the poor by sending his crop to market as
soon as it was ready, to the disgust of farmers who kept back
supplies to force up the price. O'Connor himself sometimes
worked in the fields, bridging the gap between landlord and
peasant which was so dangerous in Ireland. It is unjust to say, as
Mark Hovel did, that O'Connor had never done an honest day's

---

12. *National Instructor*, 57-58.
13. Burke, *Vicissitudes of Families*, 40.

work in his life.[14] At Fort Robert he practised the rural life which he was later to preach to the Chartists with such vehemence.

As well as with his workpeople, O'Connor quickly became a popular figure among the local gentry. Both his appearance and his manner made him conspicuous in society. He was red-headed and fair-skinned, tall, well-built. His protruding brow gave his eyes and upper face an unusual sunken appearance. His nose, though small, was prominent because of its turned-up shape. His conversational manner was voluble, engaging and often amusing, for he had a remarkable capacity for mimicry and telling anecdotes. His liveliness and humour were much appreciated by his neighbours, especially in the long winter evenings when life deep in the country was apt to be drab. Indoors O'Connor was an expert whist player: out-of-doors an expert horseman and keen fox-hunter.[15]

During these happy years at Fort Robert O'Connor did not give quite all his energies to the land and to local society. He also studied the law. His father had qualified as a barrister and no doubt wished Feargus to do the same. Feargus's own account, however, of what drew him to the bar does not mention his father; it was typical in its impulsiveness. He declared that he was once listening to the great Irish lawyer McNally examining a witness. One of the replies struck him as funny and he burst out laughing. Whereupon the usher silenced him by striking him with a wand. Feargus was so annoyed that he left the court, determined that the day would come when he would be treated with more respect in the courts of law, and forthwith he signed on at the King's Inns, Dublin.[16] If true, this incident must have occurred before 1820 when McNally died, and sure enough we find that at Easter 1819 a memorial for admission to the King's Inns was presented by

---

14. M. Hovell, *The Chartist Movement* (2nd ed., 1959), 67.
15. [J. Grant], *Random Recollections of the House of Commons* (3rd ed., 1836), 322-23; Daunt, *Eighty-Five Years*, I, 242-43, and *Life Spent for Ireland*, 160.
   Four portraits of O'Connor survive at Manch House, the best showing him when M.P. for Co. Cork. A fifth portrait (undated, probably late) is in the Nottingham Mechanics' Institution; it cost one guinea. Neither the English nor the Irish National Portrait Galleries have portraits of O'Connor in their collections: he was not a sufficiently 'respectable' politician.
16. *National Instructor*, 57.

'Edward O'Connor, fourth son of Roger, Connerville, C. Cork'.[17] This was certainly Feargus, who in his early days was often known by his second name and did not adopt the more patriotic appellation until he began to achieve notice as a politician. He was probably admitted to the King's Inns soon after this date, for in his pamphlet of 1822 he described himself as a student-at-law. In order to be called to the bar, whether English or Irish, it was then necessary to spend at least two years keeping terms at one of the Inns of Court in London. O'Connor's legal studies were probably not very intensive, for not until November 23, 1826 did he embark upon this last stage and join Gray's Inn, London.[18] In Trinity Term 1830 he finally applied for admission to the Irish bar. His application was probably successful, for in 1831 he appeared as junior counsel in an election bribery case.[19]

Feargus never became a full-time practising barrister. Soon after he qualified he became immersed in politics, and it was in political connections that he later used his legal knowledge. In Ireland he acted on the popular side in anti-tithe and election cases and assisted in securing the proper registration of Radical voters. As the Chartist leader in England he pronounced (often unsoundly) upon such questions as the legality of public meetings or of the Land Scheme. His legal knowledge was also useful to him on the several occasions when he was threatened with government prosecutions. His position as a barrister undoubtedly helped to establish his authority over the Chartist masses. They were impressed by the legal jargon with which he was able to pepper his speeches when appropriate. They overlooked the unlawyerlike lack of logic and precision in those speeches. For though Feargus O'Connor was trained in the law, he never acquired the legal mind. He was to be an emotional, romantic politician : the very opposite of the lawyer in politics.

---

17. Records of the King's Inns, Dublin.
18, J. Foster, *Register of Admissions to Gray's Inn, 1521-1889* (p.p., 1889), 433.
19. O'Connor, *Letters . . . to O'Connell*, 2-3.

CHAPTER III

REFORM AND REPEAL IN COUNTY CORK

IRELAND in the early nineteenth century was a country of many problems. At the root of all lay the problem of land. Apart from Ulster, the island was almost completely dependent upon agriculture. Consequently, the landlords had almost a monopoly of the means of existence; rents tended to be high and conditions of tenure hard. Because of the pressure of population peasant holdings were often too small for efficient cultivation. Marriages were made early and families were large. Population grew from about five millions in 1800 to over eight millions by 1840. The peasants lived in wretched cabins, and their staple food was potatoes, which they grew in primitive fashion upon scraps of land.

If Ireland were to progress she needed a revolution in techniques of cultivation and forms of landholding. But for various reasons this revolution was difficult to begin. Many landlords lacked the capital to improve their estates. In any case, improvement usually meant larger units of production, and what was to become then of the dispossessed peasant smallholders? Tenant farmers of larger holdings were discouraged from venturing upon improvement because they had no legal right to compensation for their work when leases ran out.

These problems could have been more easily resolved if there had been a less wide gap between landlords and their dependants. Many landlords were descendants of English or Scottish adventures who had taken over land confiscated from Irish Catholics during the seventeenth century. The Irish peasantry regarded them as alien intruders, the more so as many of them were rarely seen in Ireland, preferring to live in England and entrusting the administration of their estates to bailiffs. Moreover most of the landlords were Protestants, whereas most of the peasants were Roman Catholics. This religious difference was exacerbated by the existence of the Protestant Established Church of Ireland. Although Protestants of all shades comprised only about one-tenth of the total population, the Roman Catholic majority was compelled to pay tithe and cess in support of the Protestant Establishment.

The volatile Irish were not a people to accept such injustice quietly. They wanted the government of Ireland in their own hands, Roman Catholic and truly Irish. The United Irishmen of the 1790s had sought a republic entirely separate from England. The answer of the younger Pitt had been to bind Ireland still closer to England by the Act of Union of 1800. Thereafter the demand of Irish patriots was for repeal of the union and the establishment of an independent parliament at Dublin which would begin to tackle in sympathy and in knowledge the many problems of Ireland.

This was the situation of inter-related economic, social, religious and constitutional grievances when Feargus O'Connor came south and took up residence at Fort Robert. Co. Cork, with a numerous Catholic peasantry living in misery under Protestant landlords, exhibited in an intense form the problems of Ireland. 'The Tillage,' declared one contemporary account, 'except on the demesnes of the resident gentlemen, presents rather unfavourable features, owing in great measure to the want of skill and adequate capital, the too minute subdivision of farms, and the superabundant population of the arable districts.' Yet despite their miserable conditions the same observer noted that the peasants were 'hardy, active, and lively'.[1] They did not accept their lot resignedly. Secret societies of 'Whiteboys' flourished. During the early 1820s conditions in Co. Cork resembled a miniature civil war between agrarian insurgents and troops. Determined attempts were made to prevent the collection of rent and of tithe, and several leading Protestant families were driven from their seats into the town of Bandon for refuge.

Significantly, one Protestant landlord who did not flee into Bandon for refuge was Feargus O'Connor. Fort Robert stood in the centre of the disturbed district, and Feargus seems to have played a prominent part in organising the insurgents. The White-

---

1. S. Lewis, *A Topographical Dictionary of Ireland* (2nd ed., 1847), 389, 393, II, 191.

boys, observed the *Annual Register*, were recognised as nearly all local men, 'many of them comfortable farmers.' O'Connor could loosely come within this description. They showed 'uncommon confidence', we are told, in facing the troops, despite heavy casualties. Again, this sounds like O'Connor. Apparently he was himself wounded in one encounter.[2] Eventually he came under threat of arrest and decided to flee to London. He lay low there for thirteen months before returning to Ireland. He claimed to have written during his exile a novel, two tragedies, a comedy and a farce; but none of these was ever published.[3]

As well as a secret conspirator O'Connor now first appeared as a politician in the open. In 1822 he delivered his first public speech. This was at a meeting held to consider peasant grievances in the Roman Catholic chapel of Enniskeen, a village a few miles east of Fort Robert. The text of his address has not been preserved, but it seems to have been in strong terms for he subsequently claimed that it contained 'a little spice of treason'. It was probably like his anti-tithe speeches of ten years later, a confused but fiery denunciation of the landlords delivered with a fervour that would impress his Irish audience.[4]

In 1822 O'Connor also first appeared in print. He attempted a diagnosis of the Irish problem in a pamphlet printed at Cork entitled *A State of Ireland*. This was the same title as a pamphlet of his uncle Arthur O'Connor's published in 1798: Feargus was consciously drawing upon the credit of his uncle as an Irish patriot. Feargus's work consisted of a series of disjointed and unoriginal though stringent observations upon landlords and clergy, tithes, corrupt magistrates and grand jurors, for which in later years he unconvincingly claimed great influence. Its main interest really lies in the light which it throws upon O'Connor himself. His objective was clear: his means were confused. He showed a genuine sympathy for the burdens of the Irish people; but how were they to throw off these burdens? O'Connor's argument oscillated between loud language which implied the possible ultimate use of force and vehement protestations of a desire for peace at all times.

---

2. *Annual Register, 1822,* Chronicle, 14-16, 19, 35; *National Instructor,* 88-90.
3. Ibid, 104-5.
4. Ibid, 89-90.

We see foreshadowed here one of the characteristics of O'Connor as a Chartist leader: the sincerity of his feeling for the people, the dangerous uncertainty of his practical policy. Significant also for his Chartist future was the manner in which O'Connor appealed to English as well as to Irish readers. His pamphlet was dedicated 'to the People of England'. Governed by similar laws to the Irish people, O'Connor argued that the English must be interested and alarmed at the unjust administration of the law in Ireland. Also in this pamphlet we see O'Connor's developing image of himself as a leader of the people. 'I will become your advocate,' he concluded, 'as no better has offered.'

Hearing of the violent passages in *A State of Ireland*, the High Sheriff of Cork seized the whole first printing before it could leave the press.[5] A second edition seems, however, to have circulated. A large part of it was repeated in O'Connor's *Letter . . . to the Marquis of Anglesea* in 1832. This underlines another characteristic of O'Connor. His stock of ideas was limited; those he had were often repeated.

After 1822 we hear no more of O'Connor in politics for nearly ten years. He took no part in O'Connell's agitation for Catholic Emancipation, which he held would do no more than remove a grievance of middle-class Catholics.[6] We first hear of him again speaking at a county meeting in favour of parliamentary reform at Cork on December 1, 1831. The fight for the Reform Bill was now on, and the intention of the sponsors of the meeting was to support the comparatively moderate degree of reform embodied in the bill. The local Whig gentry held forth along these lines; but towards the end of the meeting O'Connor stood up and made what was to become a typical speech, going far beyond what the previous speakers had demanded. He declared himself for universal suffrage, annual parliaments and vote by ballot, as well as for total repeal of the union with England.[7]

O'Connor soon moved on from parliamentary to ecclesiastical reform. During the summer of 1832 he spoke at anti-tithe meetings throughout the county. These became increasingly large and

---

5. *National Instructor*, 90.
6. *Northern Star*, Nov. 9, 1839.
7. *The Constitution, or Cork Advertiser*, Dec. 3, 1831; Daunt, *Eighty-Five Years*, I, 229-30.

noisy. O'Connor was now deliberately bidding to become a popular leader, the ambition which he had first revealed in his pamphlet of 1822. He used the local press to puff his reputation. On his own confession he attracted reporters to his anti-tithe meetings by paying them three guineas for each time they attended. Their reports made gatherings of a few people sound like large assemblages. One report in the *Cork Southern Reporter* assured its readers that O'Connor attracted no less than two hundred thousand people to an anti-tithe meeting at Enniskeen. In August 1832 we read at length of a 'Great Public Dinner' given to O'Connor at the same place: readers were not told that this was organised and paid for by O'Connor himself. At this dinner O'Connor explained why, as a Protestant, he was hostile to tithes. 'My object,' he declared, 'is to purify the religion I profess by lopping off its rotten and redundant temporalities.'[8]

About this time O'Connor decided to attend a vestry meeting in his local Protestant parish church at Kinneigh. The curate was in the chair, and the vestry was composed of tradesmen looking for jobs. 'The first item was, I think, six guineas for a ladder to repair a little hole in the roof; I objected, and said that I would send them a ladder at my own expense.' And in this spirit Feargus went down the list, proposing drastic reductions in all items of expenditure so that cess would be reduced from $5\frac{1}{2}$d. to $\frac{3}{4}$d. an acre. Soon afterwards the curate denounced him from the pulpit for his anti-tithe activities. 'I got up, put on my hat, and walked out of the Church,' O'Connor wrote in 1850, '... and from that day till the present I have never entered a church.'[9]

The whole condition of the Established religion in the parish of Kinneigh certainly seems to have been unsatisfactory. Not even the oldest inhabitant, O'Connor told parliament in 1834, could remember having seen the rector, who was non-resident. He left his work to a curate, and even he lived outside the parish. The clerk lived fourteen miles away, 'and to crown all, the sexton kept an

---

8. *Cork Southern Reporter*, July 5, Aug. 18; *Cork Mercantile Chronicle*, Aug. 20, 1832; O'Connor, *Letters ... to O'Connell*, 3; *National Instructor*, 202; J. O'Connell, *Recollections*, I, 24-26; Burke, *Vicissitudes of Families*, 47-48; Daunt, *Eighty-Five Years*, I, 236, and *Life Spent for Ireland*, 13.
9. *National Instructor*, 151-52.

improper house at the church door, and sold whisky without license.'[10]

The fiery harangues delivered by O'Connor against tithe alarmed the Irish government as well as the Irish church. Early in July the Lord Lieutenant of the county was instructed to declare anti-tithe meetings illegal as calculated 'to excite terror and alarm'.[11] Once again O'Connor was threatened with legal proceedings. Perhaps in the hope of blunting this threat he published his *Letter . . . to the Marquis of Anglesea*, at that time Lord Lieutenant of Ireland. This pamphlet, printed in Cork, incorporated much of his earlier one of 1822; the rest dealt mainly with O'Connor himself, alleging that he had protected Lord Anglesey during a riot in Dublin and explaining that he was a barrister of good family and means. Such an effusion can hardly have convinced the government that O'Connor was innocuous, and on September 8, 1832 he was arrested.[12] Several other anti-tithe speakers were also seized; but one of them died suddenly, and the prosecutions were subsequently abandoned.[13]

A general election—the first under the Reform Act for Ireland —was now approaching. O'Connor had first come forward as a candidate for the county at a 'public dinner' held at Macroom on July 23rd. Repeal of the union, abolition of tithes, universal suffrage and vote by ballot were the main items in his programme.[14] At first the landlords who had hitherto controlled the two seats for the county refused to take him seriously. But O'Connor had built up a high popular reputation for himself during the summer. His anti-tithe campaign, puffed in the press, had made him widely known and in particular had won him the support of the influential Roman Catholic parish clergy. His engaging manner off the platform had made him liked for his personality as well as for his programme. (The peasants began to

---

10. *Parliamentary Debates*, third series, XXI (1834), 567-68.

11. *Cork Mercantile Chronicle*, July 18, 1832.

12. *The Constitution, or Cork Advertiser*, Sept. 11, 1832.

13. Daunt, *Eighty-Five Years*, I, 253. According to O'Connor, he was actually tried and triumphantly acquitted (*National Instructor*, 122).

14. *Cork Southern Reporter*, July 28, 1832; Daunt, *Eighty-Five Years*, I, 231-34.

speak of him familiarly as 'Fargus').[15] His arrest had inconvenienced him little and yet had given him an aura of martyrdom. Finally, the approval of his candidature by Daniel O'Connell, the Irish leader, completed the establishment of his reputation as a patriot.[16]

During the autumn of 1832 O'Connor, with limitless energy, addressed two or more election meetings a day, often in company with his neighbour O'Neill Daunt, candidate for Mallow. The fact that the pair were known as 'Thunder and Lightning' indicates the kind of speeches which they made.[17] O'Connor could produce, wrote Daunt, an extraordinary effect upon his hearers; his powers of declamation were unrivalled. 'It is true he dealt largely in bombast, broken metaphor, and inflated language; but while you listened, these blemishes were altogether lost in the infectious vehemence of his spirited manner, you were charmed with the melodious voice, the musical cadences, the astonishing volubility, the imposing self-confidence of the man.'[18] The following peroration to one of his election speeches in 1832 created, according to the *Cork Mercantile Chronicle,* 'a most extraordinary sensation':[19]

No! though our sea-bound dungeon were encompassed by the wooden walls of Old England—though the 300,000 promised Cossacks marched through the land with all the emblems of death, the rack, the scaffold, and the axe, yet I would suffer martyrdom ere I would throw up my hat, and cry 'All hail!' to him [the Lord Lieutenant] who dragged my country's Liberator like a common felon through the streets of the metropolis to answer a charge made crime by proclamation. No! though stretched upon the rack I would smile terror out of countenance, and die as I have lived—a pure lover of liberty!

In lighter vein during the same election campaign O'Connor flattered the tradespeople of Macroom:[20]

---

15. Daunt, *Eighty-Five Years,* I, 231.
16. *The Constitution, or Cork Advertiser,* Sept. 27, 1832.
17. *National Instructor,* 201, 218.
18. W. J. O'Neill Daunt, *Ireland and her Agitators* (1845), 133.
19. Ibid, 132.
20. Ibid, 120-21.

Tradesmen we are all, in fact, from the monarch who fills the throne and whose trade is that of *cabinet-making*, to the humble chimney-sweeper who loudly proclaims his calling from the house-tops. I am a tradesman of Macroom; I was bound apprentice in the great square on the 10th of June last [alluding to an anti-tithe meeting held on that day]; and on my show-board shall be Peace, Industry, Union, and Freedom.

O'Connor's methods as an orator were thus rather crude; but this crudity must not be taken to mean (as most historians have assumed) that O'Connor was simply a rabble-rouser interested merely in immediate effect. Certainly he revelled in applause, but as we follow O'Connor through his career we shall find, underlying the blarney and bombast, a serious political purpose. O'Connor sincerely, if simply, believed in the need for repeal of the Irish union and later in the need for achievement of the Chartist six points. He set out through his speeches to work up popular movements in support of these policies. In this context his bombast can be presented not as a flaw but as a strength. O'Connor knew that exaggeration can work up popular feeling much more readily than strict reason: he therefore used exaggeration in what he honestly believed to be good causes. He would have endorsed the opinion of a recent writer that political oratory should seek to achieve not logic but action. 'If, as is sometimes true, the orator does not consider himself bound by all the facts: to convert lethargy into will, to bring opposition out of acquiescence, to make the impossible possible.'[21]

Certainly, O'Connor's oratory made the seemingly impossible possible in Co. Cork in 1832. He came head of the poll, followed by his reform colleague Garrett Standish Barry. The aristocratic Tory and Whig candidates were well behind:[22]

O'Connor	1,837 votes
Barry	1,778
Lord Bernard (Tory)	995
Morris (Tory)	737
Hon. Robt. King (Whig)	401

21. H. Fairlie, 'Oratory in Political Life', *History Today*, X (1960), 3.
22. *Cork Southern Reporter*, Dec. 29, 1832, Jan. 1, 1833.

On nomination day, December 22nd, O'Connor had been able to display his wit at the expense of Bernard, son of the Earl of Bandon. Bernard was not a ready speaker, and he put the notes for his address inside his upturned hat. This inspired Feargus to remark that his rival had used his hat even if he had not used his head. This was the kind of sally which endeared O'Connor to Irish, and later to Chartist, audiences.[23]

Polling began on December 24th and lasted for four days, excluding Christmas day. All county voters had to travel to Cork to vote, and the poorer voters were marched in parties by their parish priests to the county town. On reaching Cork they were met by O'Connor and then swept triumphantly to record their votes.[24] Some of them had hazy ideas of what it was all about but willingly followed their priests. On the 29th the victory of O'Connor and Barry was announced.

O'Connor's return meant a revolution in local politics. Under his inspiration Co. Cork had followed the lead of four counties in 1826 and of Co. Clare at the O'Connell bye-election in 1828 and had repudiated the traditional right of landlords of the ascendancy parties to return their chosen candidates to parliament. O'Connor now went to Westminster not as a landlord or a Protestant (though indeed he was both), but as the representative of the Roman Catholic peasantry. As the *Cork Southern Reporter* commented after the election, he had risen in a few months 'from comparative obscurity' to be 'the recognised champion of popular rights, and the object of popular favour'.[25]

---

23. Daunt, *Eighty-Five Years,* I, 254.
24. Burke, *Vicissitudes of Families,* 51-52; Daunt, *Eighty-Five Years,* I, 253-54.
25. *Cork Southern Reporter,* Jan. 19, 1833. See also Burke, *Vicissitudes of Families,* 53, and Daunt, *Eighty-Five Years, I,* 255-56.

CHAPTER IV

M.P. FOR COUNTY CORK

O'CONNOR entered parliament as a member of Daniel O'Connell's 'tail'. The repeal party had done well at the elections, and at least thirty-eight Irish members of parliament were pledged to support repeal of the union.[1] In January 1833 twenty-six Irish members, O'Connor among them, attended a meeting of O'Connell's 'National Council', a kind of *ad hoc* Irish parliament, in Dublin. At this council Feargus was able to speak for the first time as a national leader of the Irish people.[2]

Parliament met at the end of January, and O'Connor took his seat. This must have been a great moment for him; but it soon became clear that, like Cobbett, another new member, O'Connor was not well-suited to the House of Commons. He was essentially a crowd orator, rejoicing in large uncritical audiences. The more sophisticated audience at Westminster soon noticed his lack of logic and depth. Some members were amused by this, others indignant, few impressed. Even a friendly critic had to admit that O'Connor's speeches were 'generally too wordy'.[3] Moreover, despite his claims to royal ancestry, Feargus seemed hardly a gentleman. Le Marchant, a Whig member, described O'Connell's party as 'not [a] very creditable looking set'. O'Connor, he wrote, had 'the appearance of a country attorney'. Le Marchant had heard of O'Connor's part in the Galway mail robbery. 'When he addressed the people at his election he said to them, "My lads you

---

1. R. B. McDowell, *Public Opinion and Government Policy in Ireland, 1801-1846* (1952), 133-34.
2. Daunt, *Eighty-Five Years*, I, 261-62.
3. [Grant], *Random Recollections* 323; Daunt, *Eighty-Five Years*, I, 264-65.

all know me." "Yes," called out one fellow from the crowd, "you robbed the mail".[4]

But whatever some aristocratic English politicians might think about him, O'Connor quickly rose to prominence within the Irish party. After only a few days in parliament he made his maiden speech, talking on the address about Irish grievances. Something of O'Connor's characteristic fire comes through in the condensed third-person report in Hansard : [5]

> They had waited for two years for redress of grievances from the present Ministry; and he would ask if they were to wait for ever, or for what indefinite period they were to wait? There was sympathy for the Pole when he rose against his great northern oppressor. He was a hero, as was also the Belgian; but the Irishman who rose against oppression was stigmatized as a traitor. If it was not to be a Union, the sooner it was severed the better.

The bitter disappointment of the Irish and of the English people with the Whigs and their Reform Act was to be the constant theme of O'Connor's parliamentary speeches both on Irish and on English questions. The people had put the Whigs into office 'with wreaths of laurel on their heads; but they had speedily withered'.[6] In a long declamatory speech in 1833 O'Connor bitterly attacked the Whig Coercion Act for Ireland. He denounced tithes and the Church Establishment and called for repeal of the Union. Speaking on repeal in 1834 he produced a characteristic mixture of loud and soft language, in the same spirit as his pamphlet of 1822 and of his Chartist speeches later: 'so long as I have life, I will agitate the Repeal of the Union. . . . It may be treason in Ireland; and if so, I shall glory in being a traitor. . . . But let the noble Lord not mistake me; I never will breathe a single doctrine, nor give sanction to an act that would lead to the shedding of one drop of human blood.'[7]

In 1835 O'Connor spoke in support of the introduction of a Poor Law into Ireland, not a harsh Benthamite system such as

---

4. A. Aspinall (ed.), *Three Early Nineteenth Century Diaries* (1952), 314.
5. *Parliamentary Debates*, third series, XV (1833), 453.
6. Ibid, XVII (1833), 1344; XIX (1833), 639.
7. Ibid, XV (1833), 900, 996, 1347; XXII (1834), 150-51.

was being established in England but a generous and humane one. On this topic he was at odds with his leader, Daniel O'Connell, who under the influence of contemporary political economy believed that a statutory right to poor relief would demoralise the Irish poor. O'Connor told parliament that he was aware of O'Connell's opinion, but rightly powerful as O'Connell was on other questions he would be 'quite powerless on this question'.[8]

Differences of opinion between O'Connor and O'Connell had appeared within a few weeks of Feargus's entry into parliament. O'Connell believed that it would be inexpedient during the session of 1833 to bring the repeal question specifically before parliament, since there was no hope of repeal being conceded. O'Connell believed that it would be best to leave the question temporarily in the background and to see what lesser Irish reforms the Whigs might be encouraged to offer. Characteristically, O'Connor, supported by some other Irish members and by the reform press in Co. Cork and elsewhere, disliked these cautious tactics. In the summer of 1833 he threatened to introduce a repeal motion himself, despite O'Connell's disapproval. Only after a majority of Irish members had twice voted at private meetings against raising the repeal question did O'Connor reluctantly give way.[9]

In November 1833 O'Connor and O'Connell clashed again at a public dinner in Cork. O'Connell declared that he wished the government would start competing with him by proposing liberal measures for Ireland to see if they could make converts from repeal. O'Connor interrupted him vehemently and then in his own speech compared O'Connell and repeal to Frankenstein and his monster which would destroy the master who had created it if he held back. Feargus called upon Irishmen to fight for 'repeal, the whole repeal and nothing but repeal'.[10]

---

8. *Parliamentary Debates*, third series, XXVI (1835), 1214-18.

9. *Poor Man's Guardian*, June 15, 1833; *Cork Mercantile Chronicle*, June 14—July 10, 1833; W. J. Fitzpatrick (ed.), *Correspondence of Daniel O'Connell*, (1888), I, 370; W. Fagan, *Life and Times of Daniel O'Connell* (1848), II, 243-52; Daunt, *Eighty-Five Years*, I, 265-66; McDowell, *Public Opinion and Government Policy*, 157-58.

10. *Cork Southern Reporter*, Nov. 5, 1833; O'Connor, *Letters to O'Connell*, 23-24; McDowell, *Public Opinion and Government Policy*, 158.

O'Connor undoubtedly hoped sooner or later to displace O'Connell as leader of the Irish people. Temperamentally he could not accept the role of a mere follower. As early as 1822 he had offered himself as leader 'as no better has offered', his ambition only slightly qualified by modesty. In an address to the electors of Cork during his repeal dispute with O'Connell, he promised that as 'our Great General will not lead the little band to the fight—I WILL'. Again ambition was only perfunctorily qualified by the acknowledgment that O'Connell was Ireland's 'Great General'.[11] But the final breach did not come until 1836. O'Connell seems at first to have been anxious to conciliate O'Connor if he could. He recognised that, apart from himself, no Irish leader had so much colour and enterprise. 'O'Connor may sometimes be a little wild,' he wrote in 1833, 'but he is calculated to be a useful man, and I have a great regard for him.'[12]

O'Connor's enterprise bore spectacular fruit for the Irish party at the Dungarvan bye-election in the summer of 1834. Dungarvan was almost a pocket borough of the Duke of Devonshire; but Feargus thought of a characteristic ruse to overcome this. Mounting the hustings in the main square of the town, he read out a letter headed from Lismore Castle, the duke's Irish seat, brandishing the heading before all eyes. The gist was that, while the duke was opposed to repeal, he would deem it 'most unconstitutional and improper' to direct his tenants how to vote. The people were so astonished on hearing this that they asked O'Connor to repeat the letter several times. But they never questioned its genuineness, and under its influence they flocked to vote for the repeal candidate. The election was almost over and the repeal candidate sure of success before the duke's agent galloped into the town and demanded that O'Connor show him the letter and admit that it was a forgery. Feargus readily handed it over but pointed out that he had never said that it was written by the duke. He had conveniently omitted to read out the signature, which was simply 'Ebenezer Humbug'. Feargus had put his legal knowledge to good

---

11. *Cork Mercantile Chronicle,* June 28, 1833; Fagan, *O'Connell,* II, 249.

12. Fitzpatrick, *Correspondence of Daniel O'Connell,* I, 412.

use. He could not be charged with forgery, and his stratagem was completely successful.[13]

As far as his parliamentary duties would allow O'Connor continued to agitate in Co. Cork. In January 1834 during the parliamentary recess he embarked upon a short campaign of repeal and anti-tithe meetings. Large and enthusiastic audiences, shepherded by the parish priests, came to hear him.[14] At the end of 1834 occurred the 'Rathcormac Massacre', arising out of an attempt to collect tithes by force from widow Ryan of Rathcormac, a hamlet in the east of the county. Peasants who came to help her were fired upon by troops; twelve people were killed and forty-two wounded. O'Connor hurried from Cork to the scene and addressed the people from a cornstack. According to his own account, the harangue which he gave at the funeral of the victims was so effective that even the soldiers wept.[15]

In the same month O'Connor attended a dinner at Macroom, and his speech against the Protestant Establishment may be quoted as an example of his oratorical style at its most entertaining :[16]

> I'll give the reverend gentlemen a hint. Why don't they get up a show-box and exhibit Mammon? They may do it very well, and thus exhibit him : 'Ladies and Gentlemen, this is the wonderful overgrown Irish giant that you have heard so much about; he is called Mammon, of the Church Establishment; he was an infant about the year 1690, but within the last few years he became so voracious that the whole Island was considered too small for his support. You have supported him for the last few years with millions of money, 23,700 soldiers, commutation, commissioners, policemen, and surveyors; so we just brought him over to show you the worth of your money. Look at the size of his arms; what they catch they keep, for he is very powerful; but there's always a dwarf with a giant, to show the wonderful contrasts of nature. Now, ladies and

---

13. J. O'Connell, *Recollections*, I, 97-109, *National Instructor*, 378, 391-93.

14. *Cork Mercantile Chronicle*, Jan. 23, 1834.

15. G. L. Lampson, *A Consideration of the State of Ireland in the Nineteenth Century* (1907), 165; *National Instructor*, 152-54.

16. W. J. O'Neill Daunt, 'Feargus O'Connor. A Memoir', *Young Ireland*, V (1879), 483.

gentlemen, look at these little animals in the cage. They are called Irish peasants. You, ladies and gentlemen, see how old they look; how feeble and bent in the knees; now, you'll suppose them to be sixty years of age, but they are not forty. But it was upon them that Mammon lived. One day in every week, and sometimes oftener, Mammon lived upon their sweat and marrow.'

O'Connor was an active county member. But activity cost money, and the attempt to keep up his position began seriously to undermine his financial position. He tried to live and to entertain at Fort Robert as if he had an income of many thousands; but in fact he seems to have had only about £750 a year.[17] Stories of his poverty soon reached Westminster. Le Marchant heard how O'Connor was once invited out by one of O'Connell's sons to a family dinner which was to consist simply of beef and potatoes. 'I shall be delighted,' answered Feargus, 'for that is just what I had ordered at home, *barring the beef*.'[18]

At the very end of 1834 parliament was dissolved, and a general election followed. O'Connor and Barry stood again for Co. Cork. O'Connor was as popular, noticed the *Cork Southern Reporter*, 'as on the first day he won the County from the great Aristocracy who had so long held it.'[19] Some landlords had used the weapon of eviction to punish tenants who had voted for him in 1832, and the threat of further evictions did reduce O'Connor's vote slightly. But he was still returned by a comfortable margin:[20]

O'Connor	1,630 votes
Barry	1,613
Longfield (Tory)	1,027
Bernard (Tory)	984

In his post-election address O'Connor, with a characteristic glance at Irish antiquity, congratulated the electors on having once

---

17. J. W. Knapp & E. Ombler, *Cases of Controverted Elections in the Twelfth Parliament of the United Kingdom* (1837), 393-94.

18. Aspinall, *Three Early Nineteenth Century Diaries*, 314.

19. *Cork Southern Reporter*, Jan. 22, 1835.

20. Ibid, Jan. 27, 1835; Daunt, *Eighty-Five Years*, I. 267.

more repudiated 'the *new* families and enemies of the County'.[21]

But although he topped the poll in the 1835 election O'Connor was not to return to parliament for long. Before and during the election rumours had gone round that he did not have the qualification of £600 a year in freehold necessary for a county member. Fort Robert was not freehold but held on very long lease. Longfield, the first of the defeated candidates, petitioned the Commons against O'Connor's return. A select committee was appointed and found that O'Connor's income from freehold was indeed far below £600 a year. In June 1835 O'Connor was therefore dispossessed of his seat and Longfield installed in his stead.[22]

O'Connor's parliamentary career was thus suddenly cut off. He was angry, but he wasted no time in regrets. He had already begun to build up for himself a new reputation outside parliament and outside Ireland. While never forgetting the Irish peasants and their problems, henceforward O'Connor gave his first attention to the problems of the operatives of the new England of the Industrial Revolution. The age of the Chartists was at hand.

---

21. *People's Press and Cork Weekly Gazette*, Jan. 31, 1835.
22. *Journals of the House of Commons*, vol. 90 (1835), 74-75, 87, 287, 320, 322; *Cork Southern Reporter*, June 11, 1835.

CHAPTER V

THE NEW INDUSTRY

THE story of the Industrial Revolution has often been told. All that we need to notice here are those aspects of industrial change which particularly helped to produce the Chartist outbreak.

The tempo of change varied from industry to industry and within different branches of each industry. Thus in Lancashire and the Glasgow district cotton spinning was mechanised and passed into factories at the end of the eighteenth century; but cotton weaving remained largely a domestic and manual trade until the 1830s. In the Yorkshire woollen industry a similarly long time gap occurred. In 1835 it was estimated that eight hundred and forty thousand handloom weavers were still at work in cotton, wool, linen and silk. Their numbers had actually increased since the beginning of the century. Handloom weaving was easily learnt and was free from factory discipline; many unskilled immigrants into the new industrial towns, Irish prominent among them, had taken it up. As a result, by the 1830s handloom weaving in all trades was much overcrowded. Wages were very low. The usual wage for most cotton and woollen handloom weavers was 6s. or 7s. a week when in work. The living conditions of the weavers were often deplorable. Engels described the 'Little Ireland' district of Manchester, inhabited chiefly by Irish handloom weavers:[1]

> The inhabitants live in dilapidated cottages, the windows of which are broken and patched with oilskin. The doors and the door posts are broken and rotten. The creatures who inhabit these dwellings and even their dark, wet cellars, and who live confined amidst all this filth and foul air—which cannot be dissipated because of the surrounding lofty buildings—must surely have sunk to the lowest level of humanity.

1. F. Engels, *The Condition of the Working Class in England* (trans. W. O. Henderson & W. H. Chaloner, 1958), 71-73.

By the end of the 1830s handloom weaving in cotton was a dying as well as an overcrowded trade. Power-loom weaving was now beginning to be widely introduced. Both the present and the future of the handloom weavers was thus hopeless, a fact underlined during the 1830s by a series of official inquiries into the position of the handloom weavers. A Royal Commission appointed in 1838 concluded that even the absolute power of the Czar of Russia would not have been able to raise their wages. He might indeed fix a reasonable minimum wage-scale, but manufacturers would not give out work at such rates since it would be unprofitable for them to do so :[2]

> The Czar of Russia, either by fixing on a high scale of wages, or by a direct command, might put an end to the occupation altogether, and such would be a most merciful exercise of his unlimited power; but the authority of the Government of a free country cannot thus control the subjects even for their own good; and all that remains, therefore, is to enlighten the handloom weavers as to their real situation, warn them to flee from the trade, and to beware of leading their children into it, as they would beware of the commission of the most atrocious of crimes.

The handloom weavers were reluctant to learn this lesson. Instead of giving up their trade they turned to Chartism, in the hope that democratic reform of parliament would produce a House of Commons willing to pass legislation to protect and to improve their employment.

The condition of the cotton and woollen factory workers was markedly better than that of the domestic handloom weavers. Certainly the factory operatives had many grievances : working conditions were often bad, factory discipline was oppressive, and hours of labour (especially for women and children) were too long. But wages of male cotton spinners could exceed 20s. per week, and women and children in the various ancillary jobs could earn as much as most male handloom weavers. In addition, factory employment was much steadier than that of the handloom weavers. The cycle of slump and boom, which was a prominent feature of the new industrial economy, frequently left handloom

---

2. Quoted A. Briggs (ed.), *Chartist Studies* (1959), 8-9.

weavers completely out of work at times of slack trade. But only at times of very deepest depression were many factory workers entirely laid off. Manufacturers preferred to run their mills at no profit or even at a loss rather than close them entirely because the fixed cost of not working them was high. Thus in 1839, when thousands of handloom weavers in Manchester were unemployed because of trade depression which had persisted since 1837, the cotton factories, including the new power-loom mills, were kept working on short-time. Only in 1841-42 did many of these factories start to close down completely as the cumulative effect of depression began to bankrupt manufacturers.[3]

1842 was probably the worst single year of the whole nineteenth century for working-class 'distress', as the contemporary term was. The Chartist petition of that year received over three million signatures, two-and-a-half times the number of the 1839 petition. The contrast was significant. Chartism received its earliest and most persistent support in the cotton and woollen districts from the chronically distressed handloom operatives. Because their distress was less persistent the factory workers were less consistent Chartists.

In the hosiery district of the East Midlands Chartism likewise depended primarily upon the steady support of an overcrowded domestic trade, that of the framework knitters. Over forty thousand frames were to be found in the area in the 1840s. The wages of the framework knitters had fallen as low as 4s 6d. or 5s. a week, a drop of about one-third since the end of the Napoleonic Wars. The squalor of their quarters in Nottingham, where Feargus O'Connor was returned to parliament in 1847, matched that of the handloom districts of Manchester. In Leicester the death-rate for 1840-42 was thirty per thousand, the fourth highest in the country. As with the handloom weavers of the North, inadequate wages and miserable living conditions led the framework knitters into the Chartist movement. They became Chartists, remarked the *Leicester Chronicle* in 1848, because they wanted 'a renovation of all things—a regeneration of the social state—a political

---

3. R. C. O. Matthews, *A Study in Trade-Cycle History. Economic Fluctuations in Great Britain 1833-1842* (1954), 137-48.

millennium. [Chartism] means better wages, limited hours of labour, comfort, independence, happiness'.[4]

This crude hunger-Chartism of the North and Midlands provided Feargus O'Connor with his main support. In centres with different industrial structures Chartism (at least at first) took on a more intellectual tone, notably in Birmingham and in London where lived large numbers of independent and intelligent artisans and shopkeepers. The London and Birmingham artisans took to Chartism as a political principle; they thought of natural rights. O'Connor's followers thought chiefly of bread and of decent living and working conditions.

As the Chartist movement progressed O'Connor became convinced that decent standards of living and working would not be achieved by the Charter alone. He decided that the condition of the people in the new industrial towns would only be substantially improved if large numbers of them repudiated the new industry and returned to agriculture. His Land Plan, discussed more fully in a later chapter, proposed an extensive transfer of labour from the new towns to the countryside. By the mid-'40s O'Connor was demanding not only the Charter but also the Land for the people.

Most 'respectable' contemporaries rejected both of O'Connor's demands. The two political leaders of 'respectable' opinion during the Chartist years, Sir Robert Peel, Tory Prime Minister from 1841 to 1846, and Richard Cobden, chief spokesman of the manufacturers, agreed that the masses were too ignorant to be trusted with political power, that democracy would lead to confiscation of property and to anarchy. They were equally sure that a large-scale return to the land was impracticable. They were both deeply aware of the misery produced by the new industrial system. Both of them wrote that if they were asked to create ideal societies they would always (in Peel's phrase) prefer corn fields to cotton factories. But both accepted that the national economy had become geared to the new industry and that that industry could not now be repudiated.[5]

---

4. Leicester Chronicle, April 8, 1848, quoted Briggs (ed.), *Chartist Studies*, 129.
5. L. J. Jennings (ed.), *Correspondence and Diaries of ... John Wilson Croker* (2nd ed., 1885), II, 381; J. Morley, *Life of Richard Cobden* (1903 ed.), 96-97.

How then was the undoubted misery of the new industrial system to be reduced. Some contemporaries thought it unavoidable : the people must acquiesce in God's will. Others feared that the people would not acquiesce indefinitely and expected therefore that social and political revolution must inevitably follow the Industrial Revolution.[6] 'It haunts me I may almost say night and day,' Thomas Arnold, the celebrated headmaster of Rugby, exclaimed about 1838 :

> It fills me with astonishment to see antislavery and missionary societies so busy with the ends of the earth, and yet all the worst evils of slavery and heathenism are existing among ourselves. But no man seems so gifted, or to speak more properly, so endowed by God with the spirit of wisdom, as to read this fearful riddle truly; which most Sphinx-like, if not read truly, will most surely be the destruction of us all.

But soon after Arnold wrote this despairing passage Peel and Cobden came confidently forward to read the great contemporary riddle. To relieve the difficulties of the new industry they proposed a policy of free trade. During the early 1840s this policy increasingly recommended itself first to middle-class and then to much working-class opinion. Peel introduced three great free trade budgets, in 1842, 1845 and 1846, designed to reduce costs of manufacture, thereby stimulating demand, and to lower the cost of living. To the same ends early in 1839 Cobden formed the Anti-Corn Law League to press for repeal of the Corn Laws, which taxed the importation of foreign corn. In 1846, after years of support for the Corn Laws, Peel changed his mind and, ignoring bitter opposition from the larger section of his party, steered repeal through parliament.

Thus during the crisis years of the new industrial society the free trade programme competed with the Chartist programme. Both promised a way out of the prevailing economic and social disorder. Feargus O'Connor shared the centre of the political stage with Sir Robert Peel and with Richard Cobden.

---

6. A. P. Stanley, *Life of Thomas Arnold* (1904 ed.), 489-90, 527-28, 763.

CHAPTER VI

RADICAL AGITATOR

FEARGUS O'Connor had known Sir Francis Burdett, the veteran English Radical, since boyhood, and he probably also knew William Cobbett. On entering parliament he soon became friendly with the younger London working-class Radicals. As early as March 1833 he spoke at a meeting of the National Union of the Working Classes, a body led by William Lovett and others which represented the same group of London artisans as were a few years later to draw up the People's Charter. O'Connor's special topic was the repressive policy of the Whig government in Ireland, but he enlarged this into a general attack upon the Whigs which was received by the meeting with loud cheering.[1] During his first year in the Commons he voted for Ashley's Ten Hour Factory Bill and for a motion of Attwood's seeking an inquiry into working-class distress. In 1834 he was active both inside and outside parliament in defence of the Dorchester labourers, who had been sentenced to transportation for administering illegal trade union oaths.[2]

Yet although O'Connor took considerable interest in English questions, while he continued in parliament for Co. Cork his main political ambitions were centred in Ireland. It was the loss of his Irish seat in June 1835 which made him look in earnest for support from England. The English Radicals needed a new national leader. Henry Hunt, the leading Radical demagogue, had died in February 1835 : William Cobbett, the leading Radical journalist, died in June, a few days after O'Connor's removal from

---

1. *Poor Man's Guardian,* March 23, 1833.
2. *Parliamentary Debates,* third series, XVI (1833), 963; XIX (1833), 255; XXII (1834), 860-62.

parliament. Feargus quickly decided that he would succeed them both.

Within a few days of losing his Irish seat O'Connor announced that he would stand for Cobbett's vacant seat at Oldham. He had had no previous connection with this Radical Lancashire cotton town, which he was later to describe as 'my English political birth place'. His intervention caused confusion in local Radical ranks. Cobbett's son, J. M. Cobbett, had already been adopted; but O'Connor justified his candidature by claiming that Cobbett was only half a Radical, who did not, for example, support full separation of church and state. O'Connor, by contrast, in the words of the local Radical newspaper, 'left the most dauntless Radical in Oldham behind in his profession of political faith', advocating universal suffrage, annual parliaments, vote by ballot, free trade, an equitable adjustment of the burden of the National Debt, and complete separation of church and state. Feargus went to the poll on the first day of the election, July 6th, but soon found that he had no hope of success. He therefore withdrew. Only thirty-two votes had been cast for him, but these were enough to let the Tory candidate in by a majority of thirteen over J. M. Cobbett.[3]

O'Connor's maladroit intervention at Oldham brought him censure from reformers both in England and in Ireland. But with characteristic effrontery he set out to pass off failure as success. After the election he left Oldham for Manchester in an open triumphal carriage escorted by supporters (many of them Irish) and flying a flag inscribed 'Roderick O'Connor Monarch of Ireland' as a reminder of his claims to royal ancestry. At Manchester he addressed a meeting of several thousand operatives, telling them that he hoped to contest Oldham again at the next general election and to be returned to parliament as the successor of Henry Hunt whose death had left the people leaderless.[4]

Having failed to re-enter the House of Commons immediately, O'Connor now turned to organising agitation outside parliament. He began in London, where he now lived at Hammersmith. He

---

3. *Manchester & Salford Advertiser*, June 27, July 4, 11; *Manchester Guardian*, June 27, July 1, 4, 8, 11, 1835; *Northern Star*, Dec. 4, 1841.
4. *Manchester & Salford Advertiser, Manchester Guardian*, July 11, 1835.

was received at first in a friendly spirit by Lovett and his group of intelligent artisans.[5] But Feargus had been used to the illiterate peasantry of Ireland whose support for reform was more emotional and much less rational than that of the Lovettites. Though no open breach yet came with Lovett, it was significant for the Chartist future that O'Connor soon turned away from the London artisans to the unskilled operatives, founding on September 17, 1835 a Radical Association at Marylebone. He intended this as a model for similar associations throughout the country.[6] The new association loudly denounced the Whig New Poor Law, recently passed, which by enforcing the workhouse test in place of liberal outdoor relief was regarded by the Radicals as depriving Englishmen of their traditional right to poor relief without stigma. The Marylebone Association also demanded the repatriation of the Dorchester labourers. In November O'Connor was one of a two-man deputation from the association which called upon the Home Secretary, Lord John Russell, to demand their return.[7]

The Marylebone Association probably had only a small number of members, but it provided an organisation behind O'Connor's campaign to become the English Radical leader. In December 1835 he set out for the North of England to found similar associations there. He was provided with a flattering letter of credentials, which he may well have written himself :

> We do therefore declare Feargus O'Connor to be a delegate from the great radical association, with full power to establish others of a similar character and for similar purposes; and, having entire confidence in his judgment and integrity, we invest him with the most ample authority upon his mission, to form associations upon the true radical principles, namely annual parliaments, universal suffrage, vote by ballot, equal representation, and no property qualification for members of parliament.

Here, we may note, were five of the six points of the future Charter.[8]

---

5. *Life and Struggles of William Lovett* (1920 ed.), 151-52.
6. *Northern Star,* Dec. 15, 1838.
7. *Manchester & Salford Advertiser,* Nov. 28, 1835.
8. Ibid, Dec. 12, 1835.

O'Connor visited most of the industrial towns of Lancashire and Yorkshire and claimed at the end of his tour that he had founded over fifty associations. To mark his apparent success the Manchester Radicals gave him a public dinner at which Feargus spoke openly of himself as 'the leader of the new radical party'. Few of the new associations probably survived for long, but at least temporarily O'Connor's exciting demagoguery made an impression upon popular opinion. This was shown by an address in January 1836 from the Huddersfield Radical Association. O'Connor, ever seeking to widen his influence, was thinking of standing at a bye-election in Glasgow; the Huddersfield Radicals urged the people of Glasgow to elect him, declaring that he had recently advanced the five grand principles of reform 'in a manner wholly unprecedented' by 'his splendid eloquence and powerful reasoning'.[9]

In the event O'Connor did not stand at Glasgow. He was still little known there, as he had been little known at Oldham. The *Glasgow Chronicle* remarked that it would be glad to see him returned for a suitable constituency but advised him not to persist in Glasgow, where the electors knew little more about him than that he had given good votes in parliament.[10]

In June 1836 Lovett and his group founded the London Working Men's Association. The L.W.M.A. was a deliberately exclusive body. On the one hand, members of the middle-class were excluded from any part in its control: on the other, only 'the intelligent and influential portion' of the working-class was to be admitted. The association was to seek political and social reform only by peaceful means and was to press especially for improved working-class education as the key to all future popular advancement.

The rules of the L.W.M.A. had been drawn up with O'Connor in mind. Lovett and his group of thoughtful artisans had found O'Connor's egotistical efforts for reform during the previous year most distasteful. They had found that he wanted to dominate the popular movement both in London and in the provinces; they were sure that this would deprive it of all hope of success. They wanted the working men, wrote Lovett, to stand on their own

9. Ibid, Jan. 2, 23, 1836.
10. *The Times*, Jan. 16, 1836.

feet, to think out their policies carefully for themselves. 'They were always looking up to *leadership* of one description or another; were being swayed to and fro in opinion and action by the *idol* of their choice ... the masses, in their political organizations, were taught to look up to *"great men"* (or to men *professing* greatness) rather than to great principles'. In November 1836 O'Connor was merely admitted as an honorary member of the L.W.M.A. He attended meetings thereafter, but the rules of the association effectively kept him out of any direction of its affairs.[11]

At this time the final breach took place between O'Connor and Daniel O'Connell. We have seen how Feargus had always been more radical than his leader. While in his campaign to become leader of the English Radicals O'Connor was bitterly attacking the Whigs as authors of the New Poor Law and as persecutors of the Dorchester Labourers, O'Connell was now supporting them in parliament. O'Connell grew angry at O'Connor's attacks upon his new allies, which he felt would only help the Tories who had nothing to offer Ireland. Finally, in the summer of 1836 O'Connell denounced O'Connor as a Tory Radical, coining the term as one of abuse. He condemned O'Connor's association with the English Radicals and gave him notice to quit Irish politics: 'He may be a Radical Reformer ... if he be, let him stick to the Radicals of England.'[12]

O'Connor replied in a virulent pamphlet which gave full play to his long pent-up jealousy of O'Connell. *A Series of Letters from Feargus O'Connor ... to Daniel O'Connell*, though dated 1836, actually appeared early in 1837. The letters were long and rambling, but they were more important than their crude abuse of O'Connell might at first suggest. Feargus denounced O'Connell as a self-interested dictator of Ireland who kept agitation going for his own profit but who had no sincere desire to press it to success, and who had been bribed by £1,000 from the Manchester manufacturers to give up support of the Ten Hours Bill. 'You know you hate me—know I despise you.'

How valid these charges against O'Connell were need not be

---

11. Lovett, *Life and Struggles,* 93-94.
12. O'Connor, *Letters to O'Connell,* 1-2; *Leeds Times,* Nov. 5, 1836; G. J. Holyoake, *Life of Joseph Rayner Stephens* (1881), 184-85.

decided here. The most important part of the pamphlet for O'Connor's future was his vaguely expressed call for a united agitation of English operatives and Irish peasants for social and political reform. This dream, which was to persist throughout the rest of his political career and to become much clearer, was just then forming in O'Connor's mind. O'Connell had never attempted such an alliance. If achieved, Feargus knew that it would be formidable in point of numbers. In 1841 the population of Ireland was over half that of England and Wales, over eight millions against about sixteen millions. Irish support would have given a valuable stimulus to the progress of English Radicalism just as the full support of English Radical opinion would have added to the power of the Irish popular movement.

His visits to the Industrial North had shown O'Connor that the two movements were no longer geographically separate. During the second quarter of the nineteenth century, under the stimulus of oppression and depression in Ireland, Irish immigrants flooded into England and Scotland. In 1841 there were well over four hundred thousand Irish-born residents in Great Britain. By 1851, after the great Irish famine of the mid-'40s, this number had risen to well over seven hundred thousand. To these numbers must be added an unknown (perhaps greater) number of second generation Irish born in England who were often as markedly Irish as their parents. These Irish in England and Scotland remained deeply interested in the plight of agricultural Ireland which they had left: yet they were also deeply involved in the problems of the new industrial England, for most of them were employed in the new towns. They usually took the lowest-paid jobs, becoming handloom weavers, labourers, navvies, and so on. In 1841 Lancashire had over a hundred thousand Irish-born inhabitants, 6.3 per cent. of the county's population, including nearly fifty thousand Irish-born residents in Liverpool and over thirty thousand in Manchester. Scotland also had well over a hundred thousand Irish-born residents in 1841 (almost five per cent. of the population), nearly forty-five thousand of them in Glasgow. The county of Middlesex, including London, had nearly sixty thousand Irish-born inhabitants at this date. The worst parts of the new towns were the Irish quarters. We have already quoted a description of the 'Little Ireland' district of Manchester.

O'Connor wanted these Irish in England to join with the

English operatives and with the Irish peasants still in Ireland in one monster agitation for reform. But his dream of a united movement was never to be fully realised. Daniel O'Connell was the accepted idol of Ireland. His repudiation of O'Connor almost completely destroyed the latter's influence in Ireland; it also severely restricted it over the Irish in England. The breach with O'Connell forced O'Connor to become during the Chartist years now approaching almost exclusively an English political leader. Yet, as we shall show, O'Connor's persistent dream throughout these years was to be an Irish leader also.

Despite the effect of O'Connell's attack upon O'Connor's reputation among the Irish, O'Connor's popularity among the English working-classes continued to grow. In the late summer of 1836 he visited the North again, meeting for the first time Richard Oastler and the Reverend J. R. Stephens, two Tory Radicals who had begun a noisy agitation against the New Poor Law in Lancashire and Yorkshire. Towards the end of the year O'Connor toured the Midlands, Northern England and Scotland. In November he paid his first visit to Nottingham, the town which eleven years later was to elect him to parliament. At a meeting there he was reported as exposing 'in a masterly style' the attempt to divert the efforts of reformers from reform of the House of Commons to reform of the Lords. This was a hit at O'Connell who was agitating the question of Lords reform; the quarrel between O'Connor and O'Connell was already beginning to influence the English Radical movement. In the same month an O'Connellite Irishman from Huddersfield complained that a Radical dinner, which he had expected to advocate Radical principles, had turned out to be 'a tribute of respect to an individual whose claim to popularity I, in common with others, do not recognise; and whose claim to political integrity (to say the least of it) is rather equivocal'.[13]

Although he was busy in the provinces, O'Connor was still hoping to make London the centre of his agitation. Denied influence within the London Working Men's Association, he began covertly to support a rival extremist body, the East London Democratic Association, which had as its secretary G. J. Harney,

---

13. *Nottingham Review,* Nov. 25; *Leeds Times,* Nov. 5, 1836.

subsequently a prominent physical-force Chartist. The main support for the E.L.D.A. came from the slums of the East End, notably from the Spitalfields silk weavers, a chronically poverty-stricken group. Early in 1837, probably with O'Connor's encouragement, Harney proposed an alliance between his association and the L.W.M.A. This would have given the extremists control of Lovett's organisation, for the E.L.D.A. boasted three thousand members whereas the exclusive L.W.M.A. had no more than two hundred. Lovett recognised the figure of O'Connor behind the move, and the attempt failed.[14]

Open rivalry was now proclaimed between the E.L.D.A. and Lovett's association. The *London Mercury*, organ of the ultra-Radicals, began to abuse the leaders of the L.W.M.A. as 'sham Radicals' and 'tools of the Whigs'. A body ambitiously calling itself the Central National Association was launched from the offices of the *London Mercury* in March 1837. But its president, James Bernard, was an egomaniac, and the *London Dispatch*, the organ of the L.W.M.A. was able to hold up his outbursts to ridicule. By the late summer the Central National Association had expired.[15]

O'Connor had kept discreetly in the background of the C.N.A. After its failure he decided to make the provinces, and especially the North of England, the centre of his agitation.

The Anti-Poor Law agitation in the North was now in full cry, as the Poor Law Commissioners began to set up new Poor Law Unions there. O'Connor joined Oastler and Stephens in making inflammatory speeches at meeting after meeting in Lancashire and Yorkshire. He told a meeting at Dewsbury in December 1837 that he had supported 'the immortal Cobbett' in the Commons and 'voted against every clause of the measure'. In fact, according to Hansard, O'Connor did not speak on the question in the Commons in 1834, nor did he vote against either the second or third readings.[16] Now, however, aspiring to the leadership of the

---

14. R. G. Gammage, *History of the Chartist Movement* (2nd ed., 1894), 53-54; Hovell, *Chartist Movement*, 62; A. R. Schoyen, *The Chartist Challenge* (1958), 17.

15. *London Mercury*, March 26, May 7, 1837; Schoyen, *Chartist Challenge*, 17-21.

16. *Parliamentary Debates*, third series, XXIII (1834), 842; XXIV (1834), 1061.

depressed handloom weavers of the North, O'Connor was fierce against the law. He denounced it in his Dewsbury speech as 'a complete unsettlement of the only, and the dearest, and the most consoling inheritance of the poor man'. The people asked to return to the old system, but he thought they deserved better than this. 'While all other sciences are going on to perfection, surely the science of legislation should not for ever stand still (hear); and while luxury is going on apace, and depravity and dissipation are looking for means on which to support themselves, let us also have an extensive improvement in the condition of the working classes of the people'.[17]

But how was enforcement of the new system to be prevented? By violence? In his Anti-Poor Law speeches O'Connor mixed threatening language with professions of peace in a manner calculated to give him the best of both worlds :

> The constitution told us that every man had a right to have a musket over his door, because it might be necessary to use it in his own defence—(Loud cheers.) He did not preach physical force; he had been preaching moral power for five years—what grievances they ought to bear—what amount of endurance they ought to suffer. Physical force would come as soon as the cup of suffering was overflowing; and, in his conscience, he believed that the cup of suffering was now very nearly overflowing.

With this mixture O'Connor roused an Anti-Poor Law meeting at Manchester in February 1838. He was soon to use the same technique to excite Chartist audiences. He noted that there were Irish as well as English in his audience, and he was glad 'to see Paddy and John Bull co-operating with each other'. Here was the dream of Anglo-Irish co-operation for which O'Connor now consistently pressed.[18]

Thanks to his part in the Anti-Poor Law agitation O'Connor's popularity in the North reached a new level. When in July 1837 he stood at the general election as a candidate for Preston, he was able to create much excitement in the town and he won the show of hands. The military authorities wrote to the Home Office in

---

17. G. R. W. Baxter, *Book of the Bastilles* (1841), 392-93.
18. *Manchester & Salford Advertiser*, Feb. 10, 1838.

some dismay.[19] But in the Anti-Poor Law movement O'Connor was still third man to Oastler and Stephens. Although Oastler praised him strongly in a *letter to Viscount Morpeth,* Oastler's praise had a revealing emphasis. He called O'Connor 'a greater man than I, a man well versed in Irish politics, a man full well acquainted with Ireland's wrongs'. He clearly regarded O'Connor as still primarily an Irish politician. Feargus was not yet completely accepted as an English political leader.[20]

At the end of 1837 O'Connor was able to develop his independent reputation outside Ireland by activity in support of the Glasgow cotton spinners. The committee of the Glasgow spinners' union had been arrested for alleged crimes, including the murder of a blackleg, arising out of a fifty per cent. cut in wages. The case aroused national working-class feeling. It became linked in the popular mind with the New Poor Law as part of a campaign by employers and government to oppress the people. The Glasgow spinners included a large Irish element, and this made the case especially interesting to O'Connor : two of the five accused committeemen were Irish. In November 1837 he visited Glasgow and Edinburgh. In the latter town he delivered a characteristic harangue, contrasting the 'five villains in scarlet', the judges who would try the case, with the 'five respectable gentlemen in black', the prisoners.[21]

The Glasgow spinners' case finally brought into the open the animosity between O'Connor and the Lovett group in London. Daniel O'Connell had a part in the affair. The spinners' committeemen were tried and transported. The L.W.M.A. quickly petitioned parliament for an inquiry into trade unions. Lovett hoped thereby to establish the innocence of the Glasgow men. But his request to re-open the whole question of trade unionism was certainly unwise at a time when trade unions were decidedly suspect among the higher classes. In parliament Daniel O'Connell, who disliked trade unions, succeeded in getting the inquiry. In the

---

19. *The Times,* July 8, 1837; Place Collection, set 56, vol. I, f.100; H.O. 40/35.
20. R. Oastler, *West Riding Nomination Riot: A Letter to Viscount Morpeth* (1837), 7.
21. *Journal of Henry Cockburn* (1874), I, 157; L. C. Wright, *Scottish Chartism* (1953), 32-33.

event nothing came of it; but many reformers feared the re-enact-
ment of the Combination Laws.

O'Connor saw in all this a good opportunity to attack Lovett
and to make progress in London. In speeches and in a letter in the
Northern Star on February 17, 1838 Feargus denounced O'Connell and the L.W.M.A. leaders together as enemies of the people.
Lovett replied with a long and scathing denunciation of
O'Connor's conduct since entering the English Radical movement:[22]

> your own vain self must be supreme—you must be 'the leader
> of the people'—and from the first moment that we resolved
> to form an association of working men, and called upon them
> to manage their own affairs, *and dispense with leadership of
> every description,* we have had *you* and *patriots of your feel-
> ings* continually in arms against us ... You have christened
> public meetings 'great associations' to meet your purposes—
> you have declared yourself 'the missionary of all the Radicals
> of London', your constituents being your own presumptuous
> boastings ... You tell the country that you alone 'have organ-
> ised the Radicals of London'—and tell the Londoners the
> wonders your genius has performed in the country. You carry
> your fame about with you on all occasions to sink all other
> topics in the shade—you are the great 'I AM' of politics.

After this episode the Lovett party still remained dominant in
London, but in the North the affair greatly helped O'Connor. In
August 1837 a Working Men's Association had been formed in
Leeds under the inspiration of delegates from the L.W.M.A. Similar societies were formed in other Yorkshire towns. O'Connor was
now able to capture these. In April 1838 he successfully launched
his Great Northern Union of which these local associations all
became members. Physical force was specifically accepted in the
programme of the new union as a possible means to radical reform : 'before joining the union every member should distinctly
understand, that in the event of moral force failing to procure
those privileges ... it is resolved that physical force shall be
resorted to if necessary'. In the light of O'Connor's subsequent
career we can see that this was mere bluff : he hoped that it would

22. Lovett, *Life and Struggles,* 163-67.

frighten the authorities into conceding reform. None the less the contrast with the rules of the L.W.M.A., which had definitely eschewed violence, was marked.[23]

The formation of the Great Northern Union was important not only as a victory in the North for O'Connor over the L.W.M.A. It also gave him a separate organisation in Yorkshire outside the Anti-Poor Law organisation, an instrument to spread his independent influence. In addition, in November 1837 O'Connor had started a new newspaper at Leeds, the *Northern Star*, which quickly achieved widespread influence. O'Connor was now well on the way to hegemony in the North. 'From this time,' wrote Francis Place, 'Feargus O'Connor became the Apostle of the North, the constant travelling dominant leader, and at length . . . in his own conceit, the master of the Radicals.'[24]

---

23. *Northern Star*, May 5, 1838.
24. Add. Mss., 27, 820, f.135.

CHAPTER VII

THE *NORTHERN STAR*

On Saturday November 18, 1837 appeared the first number of O'Connor's newspaper, the *Northern Star*, destined to be the newspaper of Chartism, the first great British popular newspaper. In its columns O'Connor aspired to become the successor of Cobbett, the chief Radical journalist, just as in his speaking tours throughout the country he had already set out to become the successor of Henry Hunt, the great Radical demagogue.

From the beginning of his political career O'Connor had recognised the power of the press. We have seen how in 1831-32 he had used the local newspapers to build up his reputation in Co. Cork. In parliament he had been a strong advocate of a free press, opposing the attempts of the Whigs to stifle Radical publications, notably the illegal unstamped newspapers which flourished during the early '30s.[1] O'Connor had learnt the value of a free reform press from his father and from his uncle Arthur. In 1798 Roger O'Connor had been editor of a short-lived patriotic weekly in Cork called the *Harp of Erin*. During 1797-98 in Dublin Arthur O'Connor had conducted a paper called *The Press*, which was eventually suppressed. *The Press* had succeeded another United Irish paper published from 1792 to 1797 in Belfast with which Arthur O'Connor had been connected in its last years. Feargus actually claimed in 1843 that his uncle had founded this paper in 1796. This was not correct; but the close association in Feargus's mind between this newspaper and his admired uncle was significant. For it was called the *Northern Star*, and Feargus O'Connor gave the same title to his English Radical newspaper of the 1830s.

Especially at first, O'Connor stressed in his English *Northern Star* the connection which he saw between the Irish popular

---

1. *Parliamentary Debates*, third series, XXV (1834), 400-3.

movement of the 1790s and the Anglo-Irish popular movement of the 1830s and '40s which he himself sought to lead. The eighth to the twelfth numbers of the paper (January 6th to February 3rd, 1838) reprinted a report of the examination of Arthur O'Connor before a secret committee of the House of Lords in 1798. With the number for February 10, 1838 a steel engraving of Arthur O'Connor was given away to readers. In the numbers for February 24th and March 3rd a biographical sketch of Arthur O'Connor, almost certainly by Feargus, appeared. 'Oh! that the breath of our *Northern Star*,' exclaimed Feargus, comparing it with its Irish namesake, 'may but equally raise the cause of liberty and freedom.'[2]

O'Connor thus gave the Chartist *Northern Star* marked Irish associations; but the money to finance the paper came from the operatives of industrial England. Feargus himself contributed little or nothing (for he had little to contribute), and yet he contrived to gain control of the paper.[3] The project was first discussed at a meeting addressed by O'Connor at Barnsley in January 1837. Its chief advocate was William Hill, a Swedenborgian minister from Hull, son of a Barnsley weaver. O'Connor himself does not seem at this stage to have shown much interest in the idea; but during the next few months he came to see its potential importance for himself. A newspaper of his own would give him an independent and influential position within the Radical movement. It would enable him to build up his reputation apart from that of Oastler and Stephens, the founders of the Anti-Poor Law agitation. Moreover, although O'Connor's harangues against the Poor Law were fairly well reported in the *Leeds Times* and the *Leeds Mercury*, the reports were often accompanied by criticism of his character and methods. O'Connor wanted more personal

---

2. A. O'Connor, *State of Ireland* (1843 ed., intro. F. O'Connor); Madden, *United Irishmen*, IV, 16-21, and *History of Irish Periodical Literature* (1867), II, 185-86; B. Inglis, *Freedom of the Press in Ireland 1784-1841* (1954), 92-105.

3. Unless otherwise indicated the following account of the foundation of the *Northern Star* is based upon articles by Joshua Hobson in the *Manchester Examiner*, Oct. 19, Nov. 6, 1847. These were used in E. L. H. Glasgow, 'The Establishment of the *Northern Star* Newspaper', *History*, XXXIX (1954).

publicity and no criticism : he came to see that only a newspaper of his own could provide this.

Meanwhile, Hill and his friends had decided that the new paper should be published at Barnsley, which was a strong Radical centre. Difficulties, however, delayed the appearance of the paper. Funds may have been short and also printing and publishing facilities. O'Connor now intervened. He proposed that the paper should be published at Leeds, the capital of the woollen district, where printing and publishing would be easier. Gradually O'Connor took the initiative out of Hill's hands. At an anti-Poor Law meeting on Hartshead Moor, between Bradford and Huddersfield, in May 1837 O'Connor approached Joshua Hobson, a Leeds printer and prominent Radical, who had been imprisoned for selling unstamped newspapers, to see if he would become printer and publisher of the paper. Hobson was interested but pointed out that in order to publish in Leeds new machinery would have to be bought. Outside London there were no printers, other than those already printing newspapers, with the necessary machinery. O'Connor was surprised at this and spent some weeks reconsidering his plan. Then he came to Hobson again and told him to go forward in Leeds, implying that he would meet all expenses out of his own pocket. Hobson agreed to become printer and publisher of the new paper; Hill agreed to become editor at a salary of £2 a week, doubled in 1839.

Hobson set out to buy type and machinery and to find offices. But when the machinery-makers demanded payment before delivery a crisis came. O'Connor now insisted that capital must be raised by public subscription. He argued that if more people had a stake in the paper its chances of success would be increased and its popular role emphasised. He therefore proposed to invite subscriptions for up to £800 in £1 shares, interest of twenty per cent. guaranteed by himself. In response to objections that this rate of interest was too high he reduced it to ten per cent. He then embarked upon a campaign for subscriptions, advertising the scheme at all his meetings.

O'Connor's popularity was already such that, despite growing trade depression, subscriptions to found a newspaper gradually mounted. Hill handed over what had been collected for his own venture. In all more than £690 was subscribed. About £500 of this came from five Yorkshire towns, Leeds, Halifax, Bradford,

Huddersfield and Hull. In its origins the *Northern Star* was thus essentially a Yorkshire venture.[4]

On the plea that outside intrusion would weaken the paper O'Connor contrived to exclude shareholders from participation in the actual direction of the paper. They were to be satisfied with their interest. Thus from the start O'Connor alone controlled the policy of the *Northern Star*. He alone took all the profits (which quickly became considerable) above the amount needed to pay interest to shareholders. Gradually many shareholders were paid off, with money which their own investments had made for O'Connor.

The first number of the new paper appeared on Saturday, November 18, 1837. Its full title was the *Northern Star and Leeds General Advertiser,* the price 4½d. a copy, including 1d. stamp duty. Partly because of this high price, the paper came out only weekly, as was customary with provincial newspapers at this time. It was 'Printed for the Proprietor, Feargus O'Connor, Esq., of Hammersmith, County Middlesex, by Joshua Hobson, at his Printing Offices, Nos. 12 and 13, Market-street, Briggate, Leeds'.

Only a fragment of the first number has survived. In an introductory address O'Connor admitted that the *Northern Star* was to be a personal vehicle :[5]

> The silence of the Press upon all subjects connected with the movement-party has been pointed and obvious; and, amongst others who have anxiously endeavoured to serve the public cause, I have met with marked indifference, and even insult, where it could be safely hazarded . . . The power of the press is acknowledged upon all hands, and rather than oppose it, I have preferred to arm myself with it.

From the first the new paper was successful. By February 1838 it was selling an average of over 10,000 copies per week, 1,900 of these in Leeds, 1,000 in Huddersfield, and over 800 in both Bradford and Halifax. This was more than the *Manchester Guardian* sold twice a week or the *Leeds Mercury* once a week. The *Northern Star* had jumped spectacularly to the head of the provincial press. By the end of 1838 sales were approaching 12,000 weekly. Then

---

4. *Northern Star,* Jan. 18, 1845.
5. Place Collection, set 56, vol. I, f.155.

during the first half of 1839, while the National Convention was sitting and the National Petition awaiting presentation, the circulation of the *Northern Star* rose far beyond that ever previously achieved by a provincial newspaper, even rivalling the daily circulation of *The Times,* the leader of the London press. On the evidence of the monthly newspaper stamp returns the maximum sale of the *Northern Star* during these weeks was probably over 50,000 copies per week. The Post Office was obliged to hire waggons to transport copies of the paper sent by post, there being too many to be carried in the usual fashion by the mail coaches.[6]

A circulation of 50,000 copies per week was a remarkable achievement, the more remarkable because the readers of the *Northern Star* were almost entirely members of the working-class. Popular enthusiasm for the paper and for the cause was kept up by frequent gifts to readers of engraved portraits of Radical leaders past and present: Arthur O'Connor, Hunt, Cobbett, Oastler, Stephens and others.

By modern standards even the highest circulation attained by the *Northern Star* seems insignificant. But the number of people reading each copy of an early nineteenth-century newspaper was much greater than that of a modern print. Newspapers were expensive items, and they were made the most of. They were exchanged between families, and thereby one copy might be seen by scores of readers. Newspapers were taken at public houses, reading rooms and coffee houses, where they were seen by hundreds. 'Amongst combers, handloom weavers, and others,' remembered Benjamin Wilson, a Halifax Chartist, 'politics was the chief topic. The *Northern Star* was the principal paper, and it was common practice, particularly in villages, to meet at friends' houses to read the paper and talk over political matters'. At a public meeting in Liverpool in 1838 Feargus O'Connor, advocating a boycott of anti-Chartist papers, charged his audience, 'never to drink a drop of beer where the *Mercury,* or *Sun,* or

---

6. *Northern Star,* Jan. 27, March 31, Nov. 17, 1838, Aug. 17, 1839; *Accounts & Papers,* (368) xxvi, 307, 1837-38; (9) xxx, 469, 1839; (213) xxx, 483, 1839; (449) xxxx, 493, 1839; Briggs (ed.), *Chartist Studies,* 73 n.4; Daunt, *Eighty-Five Years,* I, 268.

The Times, or *Chronicle* were taken'.[7] After the failure of the
National Convention and of the National Petition in the summer
of 1839 the circulation of the *Northern Star* never again rivalled
that of *The Times.* For several years, however, the paper continued
to have a very good sale. On the evidence of the annual newspaper
stamp returns, during the second half of 1839 it averaged well
over 30,000 copies per week, during 1840 over 18,000 a week,
during 1841 over 13,000, during 1842 over 12,000. After this
as the Chartist movement fell away so did the circulation of the
Northern Star. By 1844 sales had fallen well below 7,500 copies
per week, by 1846 they were sinking towards 6,000. Then the
climax of O'Connor's Land Plan and the crisis of 1848 brought
about a last revival. During 1847, according to figures published
by O'Connor himself, sales began at about 7,300 a week and rose
by the end of the year to well over 11,000. The number for April
15, 1848, describing the Kennington Common meeting, sold,
according to O'Connor, 21,000 copies. This was the last peak of
success. By 1850 circulation had dropped to much less than 5,000
copies per week.[8]

During its great days the *Northern Star* was a very profitable
newspaper for O'Connor. In 1839 it probably made £13,000, in
1841, £6,500.[9] But this money seems to have slipped through
O'Connor's hands very quickly. Accounts were not properly kept,
and the finances of the paper got into disorder. Feargus would
take out large sums to meet personal needs, including payment of
debts stretching back to his days as member of parliament for Co.
Cork. As a result, even when the paper was making a profit of
thousands there was always a shortage of ready money. The
Northern Star got a bad reputation with the printers' union for
irregularity in payment of wages. In its later years, when circulation had slumped and efforts were being made to cut costs, the
paper also fell foul of the union for employing more than the
permitted number of apprentices—a curious situation for a journal

7. *Northern Star,* Sept. 29, 1838; B. Wilson, *Struggles of an Old
   Chartist* [1887], 10; Briggs (ed.), *Chartist Studies,* 127.
8. *Northern Star,* Aug. 26, 1848; *Accounts & Papers,* (42)
   xxxviii, 497, 1852.
9. *Northern Star,* Nov. 21, 1846, Aug. 26, 1848; Schoyen, *Chartist
   Challenge,* 133 n.i.

which claimed to be the advocate of the claims of labour. Some at least of the money which O'Connor withdrew from the *Northern Star* was spent in the Chartist cause. Feargus claimed in July 1840 that he had spent £1,140 in attending Chartist meetings all over the country and in contributions to the defence of Chartist prisoners.[10]

The *Northern Star* appeared six months before the People's Charter was first published. It began not as a Chartist but as a general working-class Radical paper, giving most space to attacks upon the New Poor Law, to trade union questions and to O'Connor's dream of an Anglo-Irish popular alliance. O'Connor's leadership in all three connections was assiduously puffed by the paper. His speeches were reported at length, and he began to publish regular letters to the people written in a downright style which attempted to copy that of Cobbett. These letters were often addressed to 'the Fustian Jackets, Blistered Hands, and Unshorn Chins'. The aim of the paper was to consolidate O'Connor's influence in the North and also to extend it throughout the country. An editorial in May 1838 explained that the *Star* was never intended as a mere local newspaper : ' 'Tis a national organ, devoted to the interests of Democracy in the fullest and most definite sense of the word'.[11]

The People's Charter was published on May 8, 1838. It was the work of the L.W.M.A., which O'Connor opposed, and for this reason the *Northern Star* took no notice of the Charter for over two months. Only when the popularity of its simple six points had become clear did the paper take it up.

But thereafter the *Northern Star* quickly began to play a vital part in the Chartist movement. It became accepted as the leading Chartist organ, hence the rapid rise in circulation during the next twelve months. With its support O'Connor made steady progress towards predominance within the movement. Although the paper often praised other Chartist leaders, it always assumed that O'Connor was first among them. He was given continuous publicity as was no other leader. No other Chartist politician had

---

10. *Northern Star*, July 18, 1840; *Manchester Examiner*, Oct. 19, Nov. 6, 1847; A. E. Musson, *The Typographical Association* (1954), 83.

11. *Northern Star*, May 26, 1838.

control of an equally powerful organ. Other Chartist newspapers did appear, such as the *Northern Liberator, The Charter* and the *Southern Star,* but all were more or less short-lived. The *Northern Star* alone persisted.

The *Northern Star* gained and held first place among the Chartist newspapers partly because it reflected O'Connor's compelling personality and partly because it was better than its rivals journalistically. The range of its reporting was outstanding. It claimed in 1841 that it spent £500 a year on its reporting establishment, more probably than any other newspaper except *The Times.* It had correspondents in every town and village where the least Chartist activity existed. The collected reports of these correspondents gave isolated incidents and small meetings significance as part of a larger whole. Working men throughout the country were able to see themselves as part of a national movement of operatives with similar grievances and similar ideas for their removal. 'This is our strength', concluded the editor; '. . . The *Star* has more original matter than any ten papers in the kingdom'.[12]

From the start the authorities kept a close watch upon the paper. As early as December 1837 the Poor Law Commissioners tried to persuade the government to prosecute O'Connor because of the paper's incitements to violence against the Assistant Poor Law Commissioner in the North and against officers of the new Poor Law Unions. The Law Officers, however, advised against prosecution 'unless any real practical evil has been found to result from the circulation of that paper'. The *Northern Star* was therefore allowed to establish itself unmolested.[13]

Not until July 1839 was O'Connor prosecuted on account of the *Star,* for publishing a libel upon the Warminster Poor Law Guardians. He was found guilty but never brought up for sentence.[14] In March 1840, as we shall show in a subsequent chapter, O'Connor had to face a much more serious prosecution arising out of seditious matter published in the *Star.*

The success of the *Northern Star* soon led O'Connor to think

---

12. Ibid, Jan. 9, 1841; Gammage, *Chartist Movement,* 17.
13. Briggs (ed.), *Chartist Studies,* 375.
14. *Northern Star,* July 27, 1839, March 28, 1840.

of bigger things. As early as March 17, 1838 he was suggesting the establishment of a Radical evening daily in London, to be called the *Evening Star*. Not until July 1842 did such a paper appear. Its proprietor was G. E. Pardon; O'Connor was editor. The paper failed to win sufficient support and collapsed in the following February. In the *Northern Star* of June 2, 1838, O'Connor first advocated the establishment of a Radical morning daily paper. Two years later he developed this idea as part of a plan of Chartist re-organisation, offering to start a *Morning Star*. He asked twenty thousand Chartists to contribute 6d. a week for forty weeks. He promised £3,500 of his own. Shareholders were to receive ten per cent. interest per annum, except in the first year when £2,000 would be allotted to holding a Chartist convention, to paying Chartist lecturers, to the Chartist prisoners' defence fund and to other purposes. O'Connor pointed to the success of the *Northern Star*, a mere weekly. What must be the success therefore of a daily paper? 'As the Irishman, upon tasting the quince in the apple pie, exclaimed—"If one quince makes an apple pie so good, what the devil would an apple pie be if it was all quinces".' O'Connor's scheme was not taken up. The other Chartist leaders probably suspected that O'Connor was trying to repeat the move of 1837 whereby he had installed himself in control of the profitable *Northern Star* out of funds provided by the people.[15]

The idea of a Chartist daily paper, to be called *The Democrat,* was revived by supporters of O'Connor in May 1848. Feargus encouraged the scheme and suggested that it should be financed by means of 1s. shares, no one to have more than a hundred. He was to have 'the entire control of the paper'. Again nothing came of the idea.[16] Two other publications projected by Feargus about this time did appear. *The Labourer,* a monthly devoted especially to advocacy of the Land Plan, edited by O'Connor and Ernest Jones, lasted from the beginning of 1847 until the end of 1848. It was followed from May 1850 to May 1851 by a 1d. weekly, the *National Instructor*. These various projects and publications throughout his Chartist career emphasise how much O'Connor valued the power of the press.

During the middle years of Chartism nothing was heard of new

15. *Northern Star,* July 18, 1840.
16. Ibid, May 13, 1848; Gammage, *Chartist Movement,* 328.

projects. The *Northern Star* itself was declining steadily. O'Connor made drastic changes in the conduct of the paper in an effort to counter this. In July 1843 Hill was replaced as editor by Hobson, Harney becoming his assistant. At the end of November 1844 publication was transferred from Leeds to London and the title changed to the *Northern Star and National Trades' Journal.* Chartism was weak and O'Connor was trying to attract support for his paper from the reviving trade union movement. In 1847 he quarrelled with Hobson, and Harney became editor. Ernest Jones became assistant to Harney. Under Harney's influence the paper gave more attention to international labour movements. After the Kennington Common fiasco in April 1848, however, as O'Connor's reputation rapidly sank, he had increasing difficulty in controlling his subordinates. Ernest Jones left the *Star* soon afterwards. After much friction with O'Connor Harney finally gave up in 1850. By this time Feargus was going mad, losing the capacity to manage the paper. In its last months under his proprietorship the *Northern Star* was actually directed by G. W. M. Fleming and Dougal M'Gowan, its editor and printer. Finally, in January 1852 they bought the sinking paper from O'Connor for a mere £100, only to sell it in the following April to Harney, its former editor. Harney renamed it the *Star of Freedom;* but the support which had once made the *Northern Star* the most successful popular newspaper of its time was no longer there. On November 27, 1852 the *Star of Freedom* finally set.[17]

---

17. *Northern Star,* Jan. 3; *Star of Freedom,* April 17, 1852; T. Frost, *Forty Years' Recollections* (1880), 183-84; Gammage, *Chartist Movement,* 283, 380-85; Schoyen, *Chartist Challenge,* 223-26, 228.

CHAPTER VIII

O'CONNOR BECOMES A CHARTIST

NONE of the six points of the People's Charter published by the London Working Men's Association on May 8, 1838 were new demands. Agitation for the six points—universal manhood suffrage, vote by ballot, annual parliaments, equal electoral districts, payment of members of parliament, and no property qualification to be required of them—can be traced back to the 1770s. In 1780 a committee of the Westminster electors, including Charles James Fox, published a programme which included all six points of the future Charter. During the next few years the parliamentary reformers were very active; but they were not able to attract much support in the new industrial districts. Under the unreformed system of representation neither Birmingham, Manchester nor Leeds had members of their own in parliament; but the manufacturers who lived there preferred not to have any direct representation in parliament, fearing that contested elections would disturb trade. Most of the operatives in the new towns were equally uninterested in reform; they were staunch supporters of 'Church and King' and of the status quo.

Even the influence of the French Revolution after 1789 did not at first upset this prevailing conservatism in the manufacturing districts. Under the influence of the revolution the parliamentary reformers renewed their efforts during the early 1790s, but only in Sheffield did they attract extensive support. During the course of the French Revolutionary and Napoleonic Wars, however, beginning in 1793, the handloom weavers and framework knitters began to feel the pressure of overcrowding of their trades. The handloom weavers tried to persuade the government to fix a minimum wage by legislation; the framework knitters resorted to rioting and machine breaking, 'Luddism'. Neither movement was successful, and as a result by the end of the war in 1815 both handloom weavers and framework knitters were beginning to turn to Radical political reform, as the way to social and economic amelioration. The period 1816-20 saw the first large-scale, but unsuccessful, working-class Radical agitation for universal suffrage, culminating in the disastrous Peterloo Massacre of 1819.

The operatives were not supported in this movement by their employers. None the less during the later years of the war they too were changing their attitude. The Orders-in-Council, restricting trade with Europe during the war, the heavy burden of general taxation and of taxation upon industry, which was not much reduced after the peace, and the new Corn Law of 1815, combined to convince many manufacturers that the landlords who controlled parliament were interested only in protecting the interests of agriculture, even at the expense of the interests of the new industry. The manufacturers now began to demand better representation in the Commons. During the 1820s several attempts were made to secure the transfer of a few seats from 'rotten' boroughs (those with only a handful of venal electors) to the unrepresented great towns. But the opposition of the Tories in parliament frustrated all attempts at piecemeal parliamentary reform. The consequence was the crisis of 1830-32, when the middle-classes, encouraged by the success of the moderate July Revolution in France, suddenly became threatening and began loudly to demand extensive reform. The Whigs were returned to office and, rather to their own surprise, produced the Great Reform Bill. Having been twice rejected by parliament, once by the Commons and once by the Lords, the Reform Act was finally passed in June 1832. It gave two members to twenty-two new boroughs (including Birmingham, Manchester and Leeds) and one member to twenty more. Fifty-six rotten boroughs were disfranchised. In the towns the vote was given to £10 householders.

The response of the working-classes to the Reform Act was confused. Much of their attention at this time was being given to a movement led by John Doherty and Robert Owen for general trade unionism. This ended in the grandiose failure of the Grand National Consolidated Trades Union in 1834. Among those operatives who continued to think in terms of political pressure the cry was still for universal suffrage; the Reform Bill seemed inadequate. Yet in the final stages of the Reform Bill agitation many operatives in the new towns do seem to have caught the excitement of their employers, and the passing of the act was received with widespread popular enthusiasm.

But the hopes of both masters and men were soon disappointed. After 1832 the landed interest still retained control of parliament; the representation of the counties and country towns still outweighed that of the industrial districts. Parliament would not give the manufacturers free trade, as they wanted, nor would it pass a Ten Hours Factory Act as the operatives demanded. On the other hand, it did pass the unpopular New Poor Law. It was against this background of frustration that at the end of the '30s the manufacturers formed the Anti-Corn Law League and the operatives turned to the Charter. The Charter re-stated in deliberately simple terms the old Radical demands. It could be easily understood by all working men and this was a main reason for its quickly-won influence.

While the L.W.M.A. was preparing the People's Charter, the Birmingham Political Union, a middle-class Radical body, led by Thomas Attwood, R. K. Douglas and others, was drawing up a National Petition to parliament. This pointed out the disorder of the new industrial society and blamed it upon inadequate parliamentary representation of the people. To back up the National Petition the B.P.U. advocated a meeting of delegates chosen by the people, to be called a National Convention of the Industrious Classes.

The Birmingham and London movements soon coalesced. What would the North do, led by O'Connor? At first Feargus tried to ignore the Charter, since it was the work of the L.W.M.A. But he found that it gradually attracted widespread support among the Northern operatives. Suddenly, therefore, O'Connor came out as its enthusiastic supporter. At a meeting at Newcastle on June 30, 1838 he had not mentioned the Charter. He had delivered an anti-Poor Law speech in his best style. Ex-Lord Chancellor Brougham, he told his audience, was trying to get his pension increased from £4,000 to £5,000 a year. If the people had their rights, they would pay him nothing. And if Brougham asked what he was to do without wages, the people would say, ' "Go into the bastille that you have provided for the people". Then when Lord Harry and Lady Harry went into the bastille, the keeper would say, "This is your ward to the right, and this, my lady, is your ward to the left; we are Malthusians here, and are afraid you would breed, therefore you must be kept asunder".[1]

But then in the *Northern Star* of July 21st a meeting of the Radical Association at Dewsbury was reported 'to examine the "People's Charter", published by the Working Men's Association, the whole of which met the approval of the generality of its members'. This was the first reference in the paper to the Charter. Two days later O'Connor referred to it for the first time in a public speech. He told a meeting at Glasgow that at Birmingham in a fortnight 'a new charter would be submitted, embodying a constitution based on the principles in which they were all agreed. This was a constitution based on the judgment of our ancestors'. Feargus declared that he would follow Attwood and the new movement : 'this man would be a more powerful general than he was—hitherto he had been a leader now he would become a follower—a drummer in the army'. This, of course, was mere blarney; O'Connor himself aspired to lead the movement.[2]

The meeting of August 6, 1838 at Newhall Hill, Birmingham marked the beginning of the Chartist movement as a national agitation. As well as the Birmingham leaders, representatives attended from the L.W.M.A., from Scotland, R. J. Richardson represented Lancashire and O'Connor represented Yorkshire. O'Connor's presence as the accepted spokesman of the Yorkshire operatives was important recognition for him. He was now admitted as one of the national leaders of the English people. The sober-minded leaders of the B.P.U. and L.W.M.A. did not like him, nor he them, but they had had to recognise the influence which O'Connor had built up in the North in the three years since his ejection from parliament as an Irish member.

O'Connor now had a national audience, and he immediately set out to impress that audience with his fire and energy as a rising popular leader. Ignoring the susceptibilities of the moderate Birmingham and London leaders at his side, Feargus spoke to the people, present and absent, in characteristic exciting language. He told the meeting that he had travelled over two thousand miles during the previous six months; that he had seen soldiers interfering with the meetings of the people. 'He had told the soldiers

1. *Northern Star*, July 7, 1838; Gammage, *Chartist Movement*, 26.
2. *Northern Star*, July 28, 1838.

that if they were going to begin the work of carnage, to give him time to muster his battalions, and if 2,000,000 were not sufficient, 5,000,000 would stand up to do them justice.' This was the first time, deplored Lovett, that O'Connor introduced the threat of physical force at a Chartist meeting, 'or rather his Irish bragga-docio about arming and fighting.'[3]

O'Connor's influence continued to grow, but in London Lovett and his group were still in control. On September 17th they arranged a meeting in Palace Yard, Westminster, to choose dele-gates to the National Convention. O'Connor and the leaders of the extremist East London Democratic Association were excluded from the platform. Undeterred, Feargus got up and spoke from the crowd, making one of his most dashing speeches, lacking in overall logic but amusing and sometimes pointed:[4]

> It was said the working class were dirty fellows, and that among them they could not get six hundred and fifty eight who were fit to sit in the House of Commons. Indeed! He would soon alter that, he would pick out that number from the present meeting, and the first he selected he would take down to Mr. Hawes' soap factory, then he would tell them where they should reform their tailor's bills, he would next take them to the hair-dresser and perfumer, where they should be an-nointed with the fashionable stink; and having done that by way of preparation, he would quickly take them into the House of Commons, when they would be the best six hundred and fifty eight that ever sat within its walls. He counselled them against all rioting, all civil war, but still, in the hearing of the House of Commons, he would say, that rather than see the people oppressed, rather than see the constitution violated, while the people were in daily want, if no other man would do so, if the constitution was violated, he would, himself, lead the people to death or glory.

A week after the London meeting O'Connor was again in the North, the centre of his power. On September 24th he attended a monster meeting on Kersal Moor, near Manchester, to elect local

---

3. *Northern Star*, Aug. 11, 1838; Gammage, Chartist Movement, 44-46; Lovett, *Life and Struggles*, 185.
4. *Northern Star*, Sept. 22, 1838; Gammage, *Chartist Movement*, 50-52.

delegates to the National Convention. John Fielden, M.P. was in the chair, O'Connor and Stephens were the chief speakers. Delegates attended from the L.W.M.A., the B.P.U and from all parts of the country. This was probably the largest Chartist meeting ever held. Even the hostile *Manchester Guardian* thought that thirty thousand people were present: the *Morning Advertiser* claimed nearer three hundred thousand. Perhaps fifty thousand would be a fair estimate. Certainly more people attended the meeting than any other in Lancashire since Peterloo.

O'Connor's speech to this great audience is worth considering in some detail, both to illustrate his quality and limitations as a speaker and to show the programme of reform which he was putting forward at this time.[5]

When O'Connor rose to speak, the huge crowd welcomed him with prolonged cheering and waving of hats. Skilfully, he immediately responded to their good humour by making a joke, one moreover against himself as an Irishman. 'The man who can stand upon this spot', he began, 'without feeling some degree of excitement is not an Irishman'. Thus launched, Feargus delivered a typical speech, a catalogue of remarks often colourful and effective, often egotistical. He claimed that it was not forty-eight hours since he had spoken at a meeting at Brighton, information intended to impress his audience with his energy. He had been deputed by the men of Brighton to represent them at this meeting. He was glad to see Fielden, one of the leading manufacturers, in the chair. Fielden was not an anti-Corn Law hypocrite, wanting repeal of the Corn Laws so that he could pay lower wages. The Corn Law had been passed in the interests of the landlords; Peel's Bill of 1819, restoring the gold standard, had been passed in the interests of the fundlords. Now universal suffrage must be passed in the interests of the people:

> It is for this reason that I experience inexpressible pleasure in witnessing this scene . . . When I look around me, and see the hundreds of thousands thus congregated, what does it say to me? Why, that I for one, as an individual, have not toiled for nothing. It has been this universal suffrage, when others

---

5. *Manchester & Salford Advertiser, Northern Star, Manchester Times*, Sept. 29; *Manchester Guardian*, Sept. 26, 1839.

were absent from us, or were squabbling about mere matters
of form, it was

> 'My night dream, my morning thought'

I have stood by this all along.

Here was a characteristic piece of self-praise. Others had hesitated
in the popular cause, but he, Feargus, had always been determined.

Why had he advocated universal suffrage? 'Is it because I am a
man of blood? No; but because I look upon universal suffrage as
the only principle which can stop the flowing of human blood'.
Was this a threat of physical force if universal suffrage were not
conceded? O'Connor kept his language carefully ambiguous on
this vital point. He moved on to exploit feelings of class hostility
of operatives against employers. He advocated universal suffrage
'because I feel that the great discontent which now exists amongst
the working classes has all been caused by what are called the
higher classes'. Significantly, O'Connor spoke particularly to the
handloom weavers. The House of Commons merely appointed
committees to inquire into their conditions. Parliament would do
nothing practical to help them because the people were not
represented there:

> You will never be represented until every man is intrusted
> with that which nature has imprinted on the breast of every
> man, namely the power of self-defence, as implied in the vote
> of every individual; and, when I have counselled you, telling
> you that you had not tried your power to its full bearing, I
> referred to your moral power. Now here is moral power with
> a vengeance, which will be turned ere long, in spite of me,
> or of the most wise counsellors of the age, into physical
> force, because the people know that they have borne oppression
> too long and too tamely.

Notice how in this last sentence O'Connor contrived both to
threaten violence and yet to slip in a phrase ('in spite of me')
which could be used in his defence at law to claim that he had
never himself advocated force. We have already seen how
O'Connor used the same technique in his anti-Poor Law harangues. O'Connor was a demagogue by nature, but he was also a
lawyer by training.

O'Connor turned next in his speech to an old theme. He contended that universal suffrage would actually benefit people with property. He had often used the same argument in Ireland :

> When you do get a House of Commons, what will you do with it ? You'll take care that all taxation shall be reduced, and that it shall fall as lightly as possible upon the aristocracy of the country ... When men tax others they are bountiful. No wonder that the taxes have increased four millions a-year in time of peace.

Feargus next moved on to the Church question. Church and state must be separated. Then he jumped again to the anti-Corn Law movement : the people must not allow their energies to be diverted. Then he turned to Ireland :

> The union, it has been said, has been completed and perfected. No; my country is still a beggar at Britain's door; my country is in a state of abject poverty and slavery; and has become, under the domination of a faction, a drag upon British industry, which is paying their parsons.

O'Connor now developed his great theme, the need for an alliance of Irish peasants and English operatives in the interests of both :

> We want yet with us those brave Irishmen whose ancestors with our own were obliged to wade up to the knees in blood for the defence of their religion, for God, and for their country. We must have them; we must take them out of the lions' den, and allow Daniel to remain in the lions' den alone (Loud cheers and laughter.)

Here was a hit at Daniel O'Connell who had refused to bring the Irish and English people together.

Mention of O'Connell drew O'Connor on to the trade union question. O'Connell disliked trade unions : he, O'Connor, was their friend. But by themselves they were not enough; the trade unions should support the Charter.

At this point the thread of Feargus's speech (such as there was) seems to have broken completely. He rambled into remarks about the numbers present, about the state of crime in the country. But significantly, when he returned to speak of O'Connell and the

Irish question O'Connor quickly recovered his bearings. On this theme his mind was clear :

> We must have the Irish people with us to a man. What proves that our present meeting is great? Why, that O'Connell has been obliged to dread it. He says, 'We won't have the aid of the English radicals. There is one of their principles in which I won't acquiesce, and that is to pay members of parliament'. Really, that comes well from a man who gets £20,000 a year for doing nothing, to object to a man being paid £500 a year for doing his best. But do you, people of England, take it from me, that the people of Ireland are with you to a man, though they are curbed by the same infernal power which has curbed you.

In fact, O'Connell's influence had kept most of the Irish people hostile to Chartism. Irish support was O'Connor's dream, not the reality.

O'Connor next reviewed the state of the press. Its influence, he contended, was perhaps even greater than that of agitation by public meetings. This was a revealing assertion, helping to explain why Feargus had made himself proprietor of the *Northern Star*.

O'Connor then turned to the Reform Act and to the Whigs, repeating a favourite theme of his speeches in parliament. The people were now demanding what the Reform Act had promised them. The Whigs had deceived the people. 'We have no affection for the Whigs; they passed the Irish Coercion Bill, for which I have sworn eternal hatred to them'.

Then came another burst of self-praise. Feargus claimed that he had travelled two hundred miles without stopping in order to attend the present meeting :

> And as I constituted the Birmingham meeting into a virtuous jury for the trial of the Whigs. I will now carry it out at this meeting, and ask every man who believes the Whigs to have been guilty of treason to the people to hold up their hands—(There was a unanimous show of hands)—Let the reporters look at that.

Here was a typical demagogue's trick, flattering the people by inviting their participation.

Ignoring the L.W.M.A., O'Connor announced that he represented the E.L.D.A. at the meeting. Then he moved into his peroration :

> You are united as one man; and if you now stop, it will be your own fault. No man can have heard the speeches here today without knowing that our success is certain. Let us go on with our moral force at least.

Then followed another half-threat of violence. Feargus declared that the government had not enough soldiers to put down all the people of Lancashire. Finally, he blandly assumed that he had made and now led the new Chartist movement :

> If any man has a right to be proud of this meeting, I have. It has cost me many thousands of pounds to forward such objects, and many thousand miles of travelling . . . I have commenced the battle of the suffrage with you, and you are the forces with which I will fight that battle, even to the death, if necessary (Cheers).

So ended a typical O'Connor speech. Feargus was to use the same tricks of demagoguery, the same rambling argument, the same threatening language mixed with words of peace throughout his Chartist career. In later years he dwelt largely upon the Land Plan. But his basic theme, the only one which always came out clearly, was his dream of a huge Anglo-Irish popular alliance.

Feargus reiterated this dream in speech after speech in 1838-39. 'Every grievance that affected Ireland affected also both England and Scotland', he told the Birmingham meeting of August 6th, 'and there was, therefore, every inducement for the whole people of the three kingdoms to join in a holy and irresistible crusade against oppression and misrule'. He assured a Leeds meeting in April 1839 that Irishmen were now beginning to join the Chartist agitation. Ireland and Scotland would provide the physical power, England the moral power :[6]

> They should be the main-spring of the watch;—the Irish —a war-like people, and the Scotch—a war-like people, should be the outer works; and when they (the main-spring) moved,

---

6. *Northern Star*, April 6, 1839.

with their moral force, the Paddies and the Scots would begin to move with something else (Deafening cheers). Paddy had been for a long time more disciplined than they were, and knew better how to deal with the parsons and the army, the Scotch, who fought for the great Covenant before, would fight for their rights now.

This idea of an Anglo-Irish alliance was not exclusively O'Connor's. The other Chartist leaders had also seen its value. In December 1837 the Birmingham Political Union had addressed the people of England and Ireland. Lovett and his Working Men's Association made several appeals for Irish support. At the outset of the Chartist agitation Lovett had hoped to work closely with O'Connell, who had actually helped the L.W.M.A. to draw up the Charter. But soon afterwards, according to Lovett, the Whigs gave O'Connell control of Irish patronage, and immediately he withdrew from the movement, seizing upon the excuse that O'Connor, Stephens and others were advocating physical force. O'Connell described O'Connor as 'more bloody-minded and more atrocious than ever was Danton'.[7]

O'Connell conveniently ignored Lovett's more quiet brand of Chartism. His attitude left Lovett in a difficult position on the question of an Irish alliance. Lovett could hardly persist in seeking an association which O'Connell had made it plain that he did not want. O'Connor's Irish policy for the Chartists was left as the only possible one. Feargus had always contended that the Irish alliance would have to be made not with O'Connell but against him. Throughout 1838 the *Northern Star* denounced O'Connell almost weekly and called upon the Irish people to repudiate him. From December 1, 1838 to February 16, 1839 the paper reprinted in full O'Connor's virulent *Letters . . . to Daniel O'Connell.*

A cult of O'Connor now began to develop in the North. At a meeting of Yorkshire Chartists on Peep Green, between Leeds and Huddersfield, on October 15, 1838 to elect Yorkshire delegates to the National Convention (O'Connor himself to be one) banners

---

7. Lovett, *Life and Struggles,* 114-17; S. Maccoby, *English Radicalism 1832-1852* (1935), 165-66; Rachel O'Higgins, Ireland and Chartism. A Study of the Influence of Irishmen and the Irish Question on the Chartist Movement (Ph.D. thesis, Trinity College Dublin, 1959), 190-202.

were carried at the head of processions of branches of the Great Northern Union. Many of these were inscribed with the six points of the Charter; a Leeds banner carried a representation of Peterloo. But a banner from Barnsley introduced a significant innovation; it was inscribed 'Feargus O'Connor, and the Barnsley Northern Union'. This seems to have been the first time that O'Connor's name was paraded in this manner. Soon it was to become common at Chartist meetings all over the country.[8]

It was revealing that Barnsley should have apparently been the birthplace of the O'Connor cult. Throughout his Chartist career O'Connor found staunch support there. He described the town as 'the right eye of Yorkshire', 'Barnsley, glorious Barnsley'. The smaller towns of the North were always more determinedly Chartist than the big centres. In Manchester and Leeds popular opinion was never so unanimous, in part because distress never hit them so hard. In the smaller towns, where industry was less diversified, slump could have a disastrous effect. Thus Barnsley, a town of about fifteen thousand people, was heavily committed to linen manufacture; it had about four thousand linen handloom weavers. Trade depression and recent extensive introduction of power-loom weaving spread unemployment and misery among the Barnsley handloom weavers in the later 1830s. As a result, the town became a strong Chartist centre, and Feargus O'Connor became its political idol.

Among the Barnsley handloom weavers were several hundred Irish immigrants. In Barnsley more than anywhere else O'Connor succeeded in attracting Irish operatives away from O'Connell and uniting them with the English operatives within the Chartist movement. On April 5, 1839 he made a triumphal entry into the town and in his subsequent harangue delivered a strong attack upon O'Connell. He claimed that O'Connell had only one speech, and to the amusement of his Anglo-Irish audience he proceeded to mimic O'Connell's manner of delivering it. A few weeks later the Irish Chartists of Barnsley denounced 'the efforts made by that wretched apostate, Daniel O'Connell, to prevent the people of Ireland and Irishmen residing in England and Scotland from joining the Chartists'. The meeting of April 5th voted its 'perfect

---

8. *Northern Star*, Oct. 16, 1838.

confidence in the noble-minded Feargus O'Connor ... the Irish Wallace'.[9]

Another strong centre of O'Connorite feeling was Halifax. One man there was said to have left Feargus a house and chattels worth £2,000 in recognition of his political honesty. The followers of O'Connor in these smaller towns regarded him as a model both in mind and in body. Benjamin Wilson of Halifax believed that O'Connor was 'the founder and leader of the Chartist movement, and no man was better adapted for the purpose, he being a giant in intellect as well as in frame'. The work of the London and Birmingham leaders in launching the Chartist campaign was forgotten before the appeal of O'Connor's personality.[10]

The predominance of O'Connor among the Chartists of the North became complete during the winter of 1838-39. Until then he had had a strong rival in Stephens, whose speeches were still more inflammatory than those of Feargus. But in the end Stephens went too far. At Christmas 1838 he was arrested, and thereafter the way was clear for O'Connor. O'Connor's own language at this date was indeed only slightly less inflammatory than that of Stephens. In the autumn of 1838 the Chartists began to meet in the evenings by torchlight. Rushing from meeting to meeting all over the North, O'Connor became over-excited by the large crowds and eerie surroundings. His language grew stronger and his customary contradictory professions of peace increasingly insignificant. 'One of those torches', he told a meeting at Rochdale in November, 'was worth a thousand speeches; it spoke a language so intelligible that no one could misunderstand.' In a speech at Manchester on November 7 O'Connor decried the estimate of the leaders of the Birmingham Political Union that three years' agitation would be needed to carry the Charter. Feargus fixed September 29, 1839 as the date by which the Charter must be enacted:

---

9. *Northern Star,* April 13, May 4, 1839; O'Higgins, Ireland and Chartism, 241-50.

10. Wilson, *Struggles of an Old Chartist,* 15; Daunt, *Eighty-Five Years,* I, 268, and *Life Spent for Ireland,* 100.

'For himself he knew that nature would be exhausted, if it were longer protracted'.[11]

Roused by O'Connor's harangues, the more ardent Chartists began to drill and to equip themselves with firearms, pikes and other weapons. But really Feargus had no intention of leading an English revolution. In his torchlight speeches he went further than he intended. Certainly, his speeches at Kersal Moor and elsewhere in the summer had been threatening enough. This degree of threat had been deliberate. O'Connor believed that a noisy movement would be able to stampede parliament into conceding reform. But his subsequent career, notably his attitude at the Kennington Common meeting in 1848, showed that O'Connor was not a man to go beyond threats. His temperament was well revealed when he finally became insane. His keeper noted that he 'seemed to delight in terrorising his visitors by pretended violence, but manifested great timidity when checked by his guardians'. In this spirit, when on December 12, 1838 a proclamation was issued against torchlight meetings, O'Connor, despite all his strong language of the preceding weeks, immediately repudiated in the *Northern Star* any use of physical force.[12]

In London O'Connor now openly supported the East London Democratic Association against Lovett's Working Men's Association. The rivalry between O'Connor and Lovett came to a head at a public meeting at the Hall of Science, Commercial Road, on December 20th. Leaders of both associations were on the platform. The meeting was stormy. Lovett threatened to leave the movement: 'If the people were to be called upon to arm—if they were to go on using violent expressions which must lead to mischief, he would have nothing to do with them'. But this threat did not save his influence. O'Connor carried the meeting. During the next few weeks the bluffing O'Connorite cry 'the Charter peacefully if we can, forcibly if we must' was endorsed by Radical Associations at Hammersmith (where Feargus lived), Chiswick, Kensington and Wandsworth.[13]

---

11. *Manchester Guardian*, Nov. 10, Dec. 12; *Northern Star*, Nov. 10, 1838.

12. *Gentleman's Magazine*, new series, XLIV (1855), 546; *Northern Star*, Dec. 15, 1838.

13. *Northern Star*, Dec. 29, 1838; Schoyen, *Chartist Challenge*, 41.

O'Connor also successfully challenged the position of the leaders of the Political Union in Birmingham. On November 13th he attended, uninvited, the weekly meeting of the union in order to justify in person his Manchester speech of November 7th. He claimed that it was necessary to fix a time-limit to peaceful agitation otherwise the people would lose heart. A week later he attended again and attracted cheers and sympathy by claiming that he was on trial before the honest working men of Birmingham. He succeeded in splitting the ranks of the Birmingham Chartists. Muntz, a moderate leader, was hissed in his own stronghold, and the meeting had to be adjourned. The next week a reconciliation was arranged. O'Connor probably felt that he was not yet strong enough to shatter the influence of the B.P.U. completely. But he had established a strong following among the local operatives and had shown that he now held the initiative both in Birmingham and in London. In the opinion of the masses in the Midlands and in the South as well as in the North O'Connor now overshadowed Lovett and Attwood.[14]

In Scotland too O'Connor strengthened his position. He succeeded in persuading several Scottish Chartist Associations to rescind moral force resolutions which had been passed at a central meeting of Scottish Radical Associations on December 5, 1838.[15] As the meeting of the National Convention drew near, Feargus O'Connor had become widely accepted as the national leader of the Chartist movement.

---

14. *Northern Star,* Nov. 17, 24, Dec. 1, 1838.
15. Ibid, Jan. 19, 1839; Wright, *Scottish Chartism,* 49-52; Briggs (ed.), *Chartist Studies,* 279-80.

CHAPTER IX

CHARTISM FRUSTRATED

THE Chartist Convention met on February 4, 1839 at the British Hotel, Cockspur Street, Charing Cross, London.[1] Two days later it moved to Bolt Court, Fleet Street. An artist sketched the scene of the first meeting. The delegates met in a long room with winter sunshine streaming in through tall windows on one side, a fire burning on the other. Their appearance was sober rather than revolutionary, about fifty delegates in all, dressed in black, mostly middle-aged. Nearly half of them belonged to non-artisan groups. Yet upon this gathering were centred the hopes of hundreds of thousands of working men. This was the body which was to achieve the Charter and thereby to begin the reorganisation of the new industrial society. Addresses flowed in from supporters in all parts of the country; some of them were joyfully read to the assembled delegates. By March 7th £1,350 in 'National Rent' had been collected in coppers throughout the country to pay the expenses of the Convention.

Feargus O'Connor was present at the first meeting, but he looked ill. He had worn himself out with his hectic speaking tours of the preceding months. Daniel O'Connell wrote on February 11th that his rival was near death and could hardly speak above a whisper : 'Poor unhappy man ! I am, after all, sincerely sorry for his premature fate'. But Feargus did not die. By this same day he had recovered sufficiently to make an important speech to the National Convention.[2]

---

1. The account in this chapter of the proceedings of the National Convention is based upon reports in the *Northern Star* and *The Charter*, February-September 1839.
2. *Northern Star*, May 30, 1840; Fitzpatrick (ed.), *Correspondence of Daniel O'Connell*, II, 171; Gammage, *Chartist Movement*, 105.

6

The Convention was backed by great enthusiasm in the country, but what did it really hope to achieve? Attwood, Lovett and the moderates hoped that it might persuade parliament to appreciate both the earnestness and the sense of responsibility of the working men, thereby encouraging parliament to concede universal suffrage. O'Connor, on the other hand, did not believe that parliament and government would be impressed by the 'respectability' of the National Convention. They would have to be frightened before they would concede the Charter. 'He had no hesitation,' he told the Convention on February 11th, 'in saying that all the craft, all the artifice, all the ingenuity, all the courtesy of that Convention would not gain a single Member of the House. The strongest impression the Convention could make would be by taking their petition in one hand, and their ulterior measures in the other.' In short, O'Connor played the same game of bluff within the Convention as he had played at the torchlight meetings before it.

The bigger the popular movement led by the Convention the more O'Connor hoped that parliament and government would be intimidated by it. On February 18th he introduced a motion in the Convention on the state of Ireland. In a well-argued speech he contended once again that the Chartists must have the support of the people of Ireland. The Irish problem was not a religious problem but a franchise problem, like the English problem. The Irish were oppressed by landlords, the English by manufacturers. Despite Daniel O'Connell, they must agitate together.

O'Connor's threatening line soon led to dissension within the Convention. O'Connor tried to explain away these differences to Chartists in the country. He asked them in the *Northern Star* of March 16th to allow the delegates 'the privilege of man and wife to fall out among ourselves ... Everything is going well in the Convention'. But the Birmingham members, the original projectors of the Convention, and other moderates gradually withdrew. According to O'Connor's own estimate, twenty-one members of the Convention, about forty per cent. of the original membership, resigned before its final collapse.[3]

Inside the Convention O'Connor spoke comparatively temperately, even in advocating threatening policies. But outside he returned to the vein of his torchlight harangues. He told a London meeting that 'physical force was treason only when it failed; it

3. *Northern Star,* Sept. 21, 1839.

was glorious freedom when it was successful'. He asked his audience what it would do if members of the Convention were arrested. 'We'd rise,' responded the crowd and broke into tremendous shouting which lasted for several minutes. 'Now,' said O'Connor, 'I'll stop; I'm hard of hearing—let me hear it again;' again the assembly vociferated, 'We'd rise—we'd rise!'[4]

But government and parliament were not frightened. The National Petition was to be presented on May 6th, and it gradually became clear to O'Connor that it would be rejected. By the end of April he was beginning to modify his tone. He now made it plain that he did not really wish the people to try physical force. He began to advocate instead a general strike of operatives to achieve the Charter. In the Convention on April 22nd he realistically pointed out the folly of attempting to use violence :

> They would not commence with a desultory warfare, or hazard their cause in one battle—(hear, hear)—but, on the other hand, if they were refused their just demands, now that the Reform Bill had been found ineffectual for the objects for which it was framed—if the masters locked up their men so as to prevent them expressing their feelings, they would have recourse to the silent monitor; they would light their torches and repair to the hill-side, and there remain until the prayer of their petition was granted. (Hear and cheers.) They would not be so foolish, however, as to bare their naked and unarmed breasts to disciplined bodies of soldiers.

Thus O'Connor now tacitly admitted that his strong language of the previous months had been only bluff, that violence was not a practicable policy. The habit of making threats was not easily shaken off, however; even in this speech he lapsed into the assertion that 'the moment moral force failed physical force would step in.'

Just as the National Petition was about to be presented the Melbourne ministry fell. Presentation had to be postponed. This was a serious blow to Chartist morale, which had already begun to sink as the ineffectiveness of the Convention had become clear. In an effort to reassert its leadership by getting into closer touch with the main body of its followers the Convention now decided to leave London. The atmosphere there had never been enthusiastic. London was not a strong Chartist centre, like Birmingham

---

4. Ibid, Feb. 16, 1839.

or Manchester. Even before the postponement of presentation of the petition O'Connor had proposed a move to Birmingham. On May 8th this was agreed to by twenty-seven votes to ten.

The Convention reassembled at Birmingham on May 13th. Stimulated by the greater Chartist enthusiasm there it issued a fiery manifesto to the people, asking them if they would support ulterior measures if the petition were rejected. A 'National Holiday,' in other words a general strike, was projected, also non-payment of rent, rates and taxes. Here at last was a decided lead from the Convention.

At Whitsuntide many public meetings were held to discuss ulterior measures. The largest were at Peep Green and Kersal Moor. O'Connor spoke at both. The numbers present were markedly smaller than at the Chartist demonstrations in the same places in the previous year. This no doubt further encouraged O'Connor to moderate his policy. Even if the people were united and organised he had already admitted that they would not be able to overcome the military, and now it was plain that they were not even all united. 'Should the soldiers fire on any one,' he told the Peep Green meeting, 'I would advise him to bolt into the first house he comes to—never mind upsetting the crockery—(Laughter),—and the middle classes will soon get frightened at these proceedings, and join in compelling the Government to do the people justice.' O'Connor was now suggesting a line of passive resistance, very different from his bold tone of a few weeks earlier.

After meeting for three days at Birmingham the Convention had adjourned. It reassembled there on July 1st but soon decided to return to London on July 10th, so as to be on hand when the National Petition was at last discussed in the Commons on July 12th. It agreed on July 3rd that if the petition were rejected certain limited ulterior measures should be enforced immediately, such as a run on the banks, exclusive dealing, abstinence from use of exciseable articles and a newspaper boycott. The question of a general strike was left over until after parliament had discussed the petition.

On July 4th a large and peaceful meeting of Chartists in the Bull Ring, Birmingham, was charged by a force of metropolitan police just arrived from London. The Chartists fought back, troops had to be called in, and serious rioting and damage to property followed. This outrage exacerbated feeling throughout the Chartist world. Then on July 12th, by two hundred and thirty-five votes to forty-six, the Commons rejected the National Petition, unimpressed by its twelve hundred thousand signatures.

This was the crisis. The National Convention now had to act or to admit its own failure. On July 13th a general strike was discussed. O'Connor, whose trial began at York on July 19th, was absent. After two days' debate the Convention resolved by thirteen votes to six to recommend a 'National Holiday' to begin on August 12th. The most important decision of the National Convention was thus carried by less than a quarter of its original number. But the decision did not stand. O'Connor now realised that a general strike would not be generally supported, except by handloom weavers and others who were already out of work or only half-employed. The factory workers were anxious to stay in their jobs while they could. On July 22nd O'Connor pointed this out to the Convention, repeating his argument in a letter in the *Northern Star* of August 3rd. An editorial in the same number exposed Chartist weakness :

> The country is not fit for it; there is no state of adequate preparation; there is no proper organization amongst the people; they are not able to act in concert with each other; they are not a tenth part of them in possession of the means of self-defence; they are not agreed in their opinions, either as to the practicability or the necessity of the measure.

On August 6th on a motion proposed by Bronterre O'Brien and seconded by O'Connor the Convention issued an address calling off the strike.

On August 26th the Convention met again, but its career was at an end. On September 6th O'Brien proposed its dissolution, and this was carried by the casting vote of John Frost, the chairman. O'Connor opposed dissolution, although advocating an adjournment. He argued that the movement needed a central body in London round which it could reorganise.

In the *Northern Star* of September 21, 1839, O'Connor discussed the reasons for the collapse of the Convention. He blamed the resignations of the middle-class members, the hostility of judges, magistrates, grand and petty jurors, the threat of military and police violence, and the hostility of the press. O'Connor argued that in the face of all these difficulties the National Convention

had done as well as could be expected. It had forced consideration of popular grievances upon parliament, upon the judges,
upon the higher classes, and above all upon the working-classes
themselves. 'Chartism, previously to the meeting of the Convention was spoken of as a thing in the clouds. The light of knowledge
has dissipated the mist.' O'Connor proposed a new Convention
to continue the work. He promised to pay thirteen English delegates £2 a week each out of the profits of the *Northern Star*. His
proposal met with little response from the other Chartist leaders
who saw it as a plan for keeping up sales of the *Star* and for
reinforcing O'Connor's control of the movement.

There was some truth in the claims which O'Connor made for
the influence of the National Convention. It failed completely as
an active body; yet simply by its existence it had symbolised the
condition of England question. But the people had not supported
it, nor had O'Connor originally justified it to them, as a mere
passive symbol. He had promised the people that the Convention
would force parliament to do something. Parliament and government had done nothing and had called O'Connor's bluff.

At first the government had let the Convention proceed unmolested, not because ministers were frightened by it but because
on the contrary they regarded it with contempt. Later on the
government became more concerned, and some twenty members
of the Convention, O'Connor among them, were arrested in the
summer of 1839. From May onwards his correspondence was
opened. The Home Office found no evidence therein of
revolutionary plots. The authorities had hardly expected to do
so; they had a low opinion of O'Connor's sincerity as a Chartist. Sir Charles Napier, military commander in the North, wrote
on May 15th that O'Connor wanted to keep agitation going so as
to maintain sales of the *Northern Star*, but that he did not want
an outbreak which might damage sales. Napier thought that
O'Connor might even be bribed to make the *Star* 'abandon its
support of the Physical Force doctrines.'[5]

But although O'Connor's own intentions were not much feared
by the authorities, they came to feel that his outbursts of wild

5. Sir C. Napier to S. M. Phillips, June 11, 1839 (H. O. 40/53);
   Sir W. F. P. Napier, *Life and Opinions of Sir Charles James
   Napier* (1857), II, 27, 34, 38; F. C. Mather, *Public Order in
   the Age of the Chartists* (1959), 220.

language at public meetings and in his newspaper might lead others into violence. For this reason O'Connor was finally prosecuted for publishing reports of seditious language in the *Northern Star* of July 13 and 20, 1839.[6]

O'Connor's trial did not come on until the following March. In the interval the Chartist movement underwent a rapid decline. O'Connor continued as active as ever, but even his enthusiasm would not counter widespread disillusionment. Nor could he check the extremists, the few Chartists who were really prepared to use physical force. Their policy was now the only one which had not been tried, and they set out in earnest to try it. Risings began to be plotted. Finally, early on the morning of November 4th a body of colliers (variously numbered in hundreds and in thousands) led by John Frost, a former magistrate who had been a member of the National Convention, marched upon the town of Newport in Monmouthshire. In the centre of the town they unexpectedly met a small body of soldiers. A few Chartists were killed and wounded; the rest dispersed without coming into action. Frost and other leaders were charged with high treason.

Did O'Connor know of the intended rising? His critics within the movement, Lovett and others, later declared that he encouraged the outbreak but deliberately went away to Ireland when it was being planned. They claimed that O'Connor did not want either to assist or to restrain Frost because he feared him as a rival for the Chartist leadership and was glad to see him attempt a rising and fail. O'Connor denied all knowledge of the plot. In view of his central position in the movement this was surprising; but it seems to have been true. Frost's modern biographer absolves O'Connor from the charges made against him, pointing out that Frost himself never said that O'Connor had deceived him. On the contrary, for the rest of his life Frost always spoke well of Feargus.[7]

Certainly, after Frost had been arrested O'Connor did all he could to help him. He promised the Chartists that he would save Frost's life and to this end engaged eminent counsel on Frost's

---

6. Law Reports 1839-40, no. 22 (H.O. 48/33).
7. J. Watkins, *Impeachment of Feargus O'Connor* (1843); F. O'Connor, *Reply to Mr. John Watkins's Charges* [1843]; *Northern Star*, May 3, 1845; Gammage, *Chartist Movement*, 263-67; Lovett, *Life and Struggles*, 244-46; D. Williams, *John Frost* (1939), 199-203.

behalf, raising a large defence fund to cover legal costs and contributing a week's profits from the *Northern Star* towards it. He was present at Monmouth courthouse throughout the trial. Frost was sentenced to hanging, drawing and quartering but was subsequently reprieved and transported for life.

One reason why O'Connor went to Ireland in October 1839 was to look to his Fort Robert estate, which he had not visited since 1836. His chief reason for going, however, was to try to establish Chartism there. Because of O'Connell's hostility the movement had made little progress in Ireland. The National Convention had sent a delegate to Dublin in August 1839, but he had been roughly handled and had achieved nothing. Feargus set out in the first instance to rouse his own county of Cork, as he had roused it in 1831-32. On October 13th he addressed a meeting in the Roman Catholic chapel at Enniskeen, near Fort Robert. 'Universal suffrage is the battle that your order in England and Scotland are now fighting; and it is the next battle that you must fight, and you shall fight with me at your head'. This was characteristic O'Connor. But his confidence could not break the power of O'Connell in Ireland. Although he addressed at least two other meetings in Co. Cork, he was not able to win it for Chartism. Reporting on his tour in the *Northern Star,* O'Connor came as near as his temperament would allow to admitting this. He assured his readers that the Irish were 'Chartists to a man. That is, they are for the five great principles, but they do not approve of the picture of Chartism, as drawn by O'Connell and his tools'.[8]

O'Connor's trial for seditious libels published in the *Northern Star* began at York on March 17, 1840. In the number for July 20, 1839 had appeared a report of a speech by William Taylor at Manchester in which he had told the people that they would soon have the chance to seize their rights by force; in the same number was printed a speech by O'Brien at Stockport urging the people to arm. The paper for July 13th had published resolutions passed at a Newcastle meeting referring to the Birmingham Bull Ring outrage and asserting that if the government insisted on using force the people would be entitled to reply with force. In the same number appeared a report of a violent

8. *Northern Star,* Aug. 17, Oct. 5—Nov. 9, 1839.

speech by O'Connor himself at Rochdale making this same point. He had also declared that

> the land belonged to the people; those who by their capital and labour cultivate it. The labourers ought to possess the earth ... But as for soldiers, police judges, barristers, bishops, and parsons, they swarmed, in this unhappy country, like locusts, devouring every green thing, and making that which should be a paradise, no better than a hell upon earth.

O'Connor's speech in his own defence, which took five hours, was a rambling and largely irrelevant political harangue. He claimed that he had always advocated only moral force, but he could make no real answer to the specific charges against him. What had appeared in his paper could not be gainsaid. Perhaps the most interesting part of his defence was his comparison of the attitude of the Whigs to himself and to Daniel O'Connell. He quoted nine extracts from speeches by O'Connell inciting the Irish people to resistance to the authorities; Feargus remarked that the Whig government had not dared to prosecute O'Connell because its existence depended upon the votes of his party in parliament. The point was not a good one, however, since the speeches in question must have dated from before O'Connell's alliance with the Whigs in 1835, when they did not in fact depend upon Irish support; after making the alliance O'Connell moderated his language. But O'Connor's use of this line of defence revealed how much he compared himself with and envied Daniel O'Connell. He returned to it in May when speaking in mitigation of sentence. The court, however, was unimpressed, and he was sentenced to eighteen months imprisonment. He had also to provide sureties, himself in £300 and two others in £150, for good behaviour for two years thereafter. Outside Chartist circles O'Connor was thought lucky, after all his strong language during 1838-39, to have escaped prosecution on a more serious charge and a more severe sentence. This was the view, for example of *The Globe* newspaper, which thought, however, that eighteen months confinement would be long enough to destroy O'Connor's popularity : 'before the expiration of the sentence Mr. Feargus O'Connor will probably be forgotten.' This was precisely what Feargus did not intend to let happen.[9]

---

9. Ibid, March 21, May 16; *The Globe*, May 13, 1840.

CHAPTER X

CHARTIST CHAMPION

DURING the first phase of the Chartist movement Feargus O'Connor, although he had made himself the most outstanding of the Chartist leaders, had still been first among several. While in prison he was able skilfully to build up a climate of Chartist opinion which generally accepted him as the sole national Chartist leader.

From his first day in jail Feargus began through the *Northern Star* to surround himself with an aura of martyrdom. Other imprisoned Chartist leaders suffered more privation in prison, but much less was heard about them. Feargus had been ill and delirious just before coming up for sentence. In a farewell letter to the Chartists written just before entering prison he suggested that life there would probably kill him : [1]

> I desire that no horse shall draw me to my resting-place, but that I shall be carried upon the shoulders of working men from the prison-house to the house of death, and then all my advice will be followed as though I had been inspired. I desire that no Whig shall be allowed to follow my remains, for it is not meet that they be murderers and mourners.

In a letter from prison published in the *Northern Star* of May 23rd Feargus complained that he had been put in a dark cold cell alongside convicted felons and offered only coarse food. This was the first of a continuous series of complaints which went on throughout his imprisonment.

The Chartists quickly responded to O'Connor's prompting. During the next few weeks petitions were sent up to parliament from many towns denouncing his treatment. Two private letters about prison conditions from O'Connor to Serjeant Talfourd,

---

1. *Northern Star*, May 16, 1840.

M.P., are preserved in the Castle Museum at York. He told Talfourd that although convicted only for a misdemeanour his sole privilege beyond that of felons was wearing his own clothes. He had presented without result two affidavits from doctors declaring that the usual prison routine would have dangerous effects upon him because of his poor health. He asked to be transferred to the Queen's Bench prison in London, near his physicians and his friends. He complained that he was not allowed books, newspapers, chair, table 'or anything to pass the time.'

The question of O'Connor's treatment in prison was brought up by the Radicals in the House of Commons on May 27, 1840. It emerged that there was some slight substance in O'Connor's complaints, and the Home Secretary intervened with the York magistrates to secure better treatment for him. The prison governor reported to parliament on July 8th that Feargus was now in the best room in the jail, that he found his own food, furniture, coal and candles, had a spacious yard to walk in, was allowed pen, ink and paper, books and newspapers, and that he was visited by his friends and had a turnkey to wait upon him.[2]

Without free use of pen and ink O'Connor could not have publicised his martyrdom and controlled the Chartist movement from inside prison. The first of his prison letters appeared in the *Northern Star* of May 23rd. Thereafter every week throughout his confinement he wrote at least one letter for publication in the paper. Often he wrote much more; the *Northern Star* of July 11, 1840, for example, carried more than a page of material from his pen. Imprisonment silenced his rivals, but O'Connor could still speak.

On July 23, 1840, a meeting of delegates assembled at Manchester to undertake a reorganisation of the Chartist movement. Various schemes were discussed. From prison O'Connor submitted a plan for a daily newspaper, which has already been mentioned. Eventually the National Charter Association was formed. This body was to dominate the Chartist movement for the rest of its existence as a significant political force. Its basis was a system of class-meetings modelled upon the example of early Methodism.

---

2. *Parliamentary Debates,* third series, LIV (1840), 647-56, 908-13, 917-22, 953-54, 1365-68; *Accounts & Papers,* (600), 1840, p.35.

O'Connor was not an officer of the N.C.A., but upon his release from prison he quickly came to dominate the new body.

O'Connor strongly opposed three other schemes of Chartist propaganda which were launched about this time. Lovett produced a scheme for educational Chartism, based upon a network of Chartist schools and libraries. Henry Vincent advocated temperence Chartism. Other Chartists began to open Chartist churches in which political sermons were preached each Sunday. O'Connor disliked these movements which smacked of middle-class methods. He argued that Church Chartism identified Chartism with one particular creed, and that teetotal Chartism implied that those who drank could not be true Chartists : 'I object to knowledge Chartism, because it impliedly acknowledges a standard of some sort of learning, education, or information as a necessary qualification to entitle man to his political rights.'[3]

O'Connor disliked Lovett and his education plan, but he hated Daniel O'Connell. At the end of 1840 it was announced that O'Connell proposed to visit Leeds to speak at a meeting on January 21, 1841 arranged by the local middle-class Radicals. This meeting was intended to establish a middle- and working-class alliance for reform. From prison O'Connor denounced the proposal as another piece of O'Connellite trickery and called upon the Yorkshire Chartists to demonstrate their loyalty to himself and their hostility to O'Connell :

> Have I not travelled night and day to relieve the captive, thousands of miles in the depth of winter! while, in return, I ask of you but *one*, one, ONE, *only* ONE *day*, devoted to your own cause and my defence. Shall my oppressor triumph over his victim—your unpaid, untiring, unpurchasable, unflinching friend, in a felon's dungeon, while you look upon the treason, and cheer the traitor in his attempt!
>
> No, no—a million times NO! I live and reign in the hearts of millions, who pant for an opportunity to prove their love, and who will embrace that which is now presented, to convince me of their approbation of my honest endeavours to serve the cause of universal freedom.
>
> I am,
> My friends and brethren,

3. *Northern Star*, April 3—May 8, 1841.

The Tyrants' captive,
The oppressors' dread,
The poor man's friend,
And the people's accepted present,
FEARGUS O'CONNOR

Nothing indicated more clearly than this letter how much O'Connorite Chartism meant hatred of Daniel O'Connell. A West Riding 'Welcome to Dan' committee was formed to organise a counter-demonstration on Holbeck Moor, Leeds. Delegates attended this meeting from all parts of the country. Chartists who had bought tickets then went to the middle-class Radical meeting, held in Marshall's mill. Joseph Hume and others spoke in favour of household suffrage. But to the dismay of the middle-class reformers O'Connell prudently decided at the last minute not to come. O'Connell knew that the *Northern Star* had reminded the Chartists of the violence shown to a Chartist missionary sent to Dublin in 1839. Household suffrage was voted down at the meeting, which ended with three cheers for O'Connor and three groans for O'Connell.[4]

O'Connor thus won a striking victory over O'Connell. He seems to have succeeded in attracting many of the fifteen thousand Irish immigrants in the West Riding in 1841 into the Chartist movement and away from O'Connell. In Lancashire, however, which had over a hundred thousand Irish-born residents in 1841, he was much less successful. In Manchester, for example, the O'Connellite Irish heavily outnumbered the O'Connorites. O'Connell supported the Anti-Corn Law League, which had its headquarters in Manchester: O'Connor opposed the League. Round the question of the Corn Laws several serious clashes occurred between English and Irish O'Connorite Chartists and O'Connellite Leaguers, organised in an Operative Anti-Corn Law Association. The most serious of these clashes took place in March 1842 when O'Connor himself was in Manchester to give a lecture. The Anti-Corn Law League arranged an O'Connellite Irish intrusion. The Chartists named a chairman, the O'Connellites insisted on one of their own number. Neither side would give way. We have accounts from both sides of what then happened. First

---

4. Ibid, Dec. 19, 1840—Jan. 23, 1841; *Leeds Times*, Jan. 23, 1841.

the version of Edward Watkin, one of the organisers of the Operative Anti-Corn Law Association, writing to Richard Cobden :[5]

> The result was a tremendous fight—all the furniture was smashed to atoms; forms—desks—chairs—gas pipes— were used as weapons & the result is something like as follows— 'The lion'—the king of Chartism—F. O'C.—knocked down 3 times—has he says 7 wounds—six he can tell the position of —the 7th. was I believe inflicted as he was running away— wh. he did after fighting about two minutes . . . 4 of the 'lambs' [i.e. O'Connellite Irish] badly hurt—2 of their sculls fractured —they however are *used to it* & will soon be well.

And now, by contrast, O'Connor's own version in the *Northern Star:*[6]

> In less than half a minute, the mahogany tables, chairs, gas pipes, and every available article was in pieces . . . The missiles now began to fly in all directions at those on the platform, when I went in front, took off my hat, and cheered the Chartists on . . . I received a blow of a large stone on the left shin, that knocked me down on a bench. I got up, and saw stones, from a pound to three pound weight, pieces of iron and missiles of every description began to fly round me . . . I received a blow of some sharp instrument behind, which cut my hat through, and as I fronted the meeting again, I received a tremendous blow from a large stone just above the right eye, which knocked me down, the blood gushing out copiously. Higginbottom and Whittaker, and two or three lifted me up and dragged me off the platform. Higginbottom and Whittaker took me into a public house, where I washed the blood off and then we proceeded to my hotel.

The emphatically Lancastrian surnames of O'Connor's assistants contrasted significantly with the Irishness of his assailants. Outside Yorkshire O'Connor's dream of an Anglo-Irish working-class alliance was far from realisation.

In Ireland itself Chartism still made little progress. In August 1841 the Irish Universal Suffrage Association was formed in

---

5. N. McCord, *The Anti-Corn Law League* (1958), 102-3.
6. *Northern Star*, March 12, 1842; *National Instructor*, 266, 279.

Dublin. A branch was established in Belfast and a few attempts were made elsewhere. Its leader was Patrick O'Higgins, a personal friend of O'Connor, whom it was rumoured at one time was to marry Feargus's sister. The *Northern Star* gave much prominence to the activities of the Irish Chartists, but the I.U.S.A. never had more than a thousand members. Daniel O'Connell retained the political leadership of Ireland.[7]

In the summer of 1841, while O'Connor was still in prison, a general election took place. In the *Northern Star* Feargus advised the Chartists to support the Tories rather than the Whigs, who had deceived the people.[8] His advice was widely followed. On this question of election tactics a serious difference of opinion developed between O'Connor and Bronterre O'Brien, another Irishman and the most intellectually able of the Chartist leaders. O'Brien, whom O'Connor had dubbed the 'Chartist School-master,' had contributed well-argued weekly articles to the early numbers of the *Northern Star*. O'Brien contended that the Chartists should support neither Whigs nor Tories at the general election, except where alliance with one party or the other might lead to the return of a Chartist candidate. These differences in 1841 between O'Connor and O'Brien were followed early next year by an open quarrel, when O'Brien came out strongly in support of the Complete Suffrage movement.

O'Connor had quarrelled in turn with Lovett and the London party, with Attwood and the Birmingham group and now with O'Brien. In each instance the Chartist masses followed O'Connor. One by one the intellectuals who had originally formulated Chartist principles were driven from the leadership, leaving only O'Connor. By 1842 O'Connor was the only generally accepted Chartist leader of the first rank. Almost all the prominent local leaders were his lieutenants, through whom he controlled the 'localities' of the National Charter Association. One of these was Thomas Cooper of Leicester who had been much impressed by O'Connor's oratory and by his letters in the *Northern Star*. Cooper believed at this time that O'Connor was 'the only really disin-terested and incorruptible leader . . . 'I opposed James Bronterre O'Brien, and Henry Vincent, and all who opposed O'Connor, or

---

7. O'Higgins, Ireland and Chartism, 102-47; Cooper, *Life*, 227.
8. *Northern Star*, May 29—June 26, 1841.

refused to act with him . . . I stuck by O'Connor, and would have gone through fire and water for him.'[9]

On August 30, 1841 O'Connor was released from prison, over two months early because of ill-health. His reappearance in public was carefully stage-managed. Over fifty Chartist delegates were sent from all parts of the country to welcome him as he came out of York Castle. He appeared in a working man's suit of fustian. He told the people outside the castle that he wore the suit to convince them 'at a single glance, that what I was when I left you, the same do I return to you.' He then set off in procession in a triumphal coach of green and pink shaped like a sea-shell. In his speech at a meeting of welcome he immediately returned to his dream of an Anglo-Irish working-class alliance, emphasising how if Ireland were made prosperous English working men would benefit : 'Justice to Ireland means higher wages, less competition, and more comforts in England . . . If Ireland's rags were six times less, your production must be six times more.'[10]

On September 11th the *Northern Star* published the words of 'The Lion of Freedom', which when set to music quickly became the song of Chartism:

> The lion of freedom comes from his den,
> We'll rally around him again and again,
> We'll crown him with laurels our champion to be,
> O'Connor, the patriot of sweet liberty.

> The pride of the nation, he's noble and brave
> He's the terror of tyrants, the friend of the slave,
> The bright star of freedom, the noblest of men,
> We'll rally around him again and again.

> Though proud daring tyrants his body confined,
> They never could alter his generous mind;
> We'll hail our caged lion, now free from his den,
> And we'll rally around him again and again.

> Who strove for the patriots? was up night and day?
> And saved them from falling to tyrants a prey?
> It was Feargus O'Connor was diligent then!
> We'll rally around him again and again.

---

9. Cooper, *Life*, 175-76, 179-80; Gammage, *Chartist Movement*, 203-5, 407-8.

10. *Northern Star*, Sept. 4, 1841.

Henceforward O'Connor was usually welcomed with this song at Chartist meetings.[11]

In the months after his release from prison O'Connor travelled indefatigably to receive the applause of meetings throughout the industrial districts. In town after town he processed in triumphal coaches surrounded by flags and banners. His reception at these meetings proved the success of his prison campaign to build up his reputation as the one Chartist leader and martyr.

We may take as our example of such a meeting that at Nottingham on February 21, 1842, described in the local Radical newspaper, the *Nottingham Review*. The paper's description of the occasion will remind us how O'Connor's personality made Chartism into a living movement, noisy and vulgar but very real. Despite rain Nottingham was early bustling and excited :

The Market-place was thronged with people, while from the different villages round, and from the distant places, processions kept coming in ... Much as the sight of so many thousands of Englishmen coming to press forward in the contest for the suffrage, might gladden the hearts of true lovers of liberty, yet, their wan and famine-like appearance, mingled with their jaded walk, and wet, forlorn condition, could not but excite a feeling of regret and sorrow in their behalf. One thing it proved—that an Englishman never forgets a friend who has laboured in his behalf—perhaps not wisely—but too well. The heroism of some hundreds coming from Mansfield, Sutton-in-Ashfield, Mansfield Woodhouse, and other distant places, all on foot, bespoke with great truth the fast hold that O'Connor had secured in the hearts of the people. It was not till near twelve o'clock that the whole of the numerous flags, devices, carriages, &c. were got in order to form the procession, and they then proceeded down Wheelergate, to the railway station, where Mr. O'Connor was received from the Birmingham train, amid immense cheering. [The spread of railways during the 1840s greatly helped O'Connor in his countrywide speaking tours]. Having taken his stand in a carriage drawn by four greys, with postillions, the procession moved into the town ... The procession was an exceedingly good one, and the flags valuable as well as numerous. First came a man mounted on a grey horse, with the Chartist colours (green) tied over it, and marshalling the way. Next came four beautiful green

11. Cooper, *Life*, 175-76; Gammage, *Chartist Movement*, 407, 409.

wreaths, suspended from an upright pole with cross-bars, and then a large green silk flag bearing the inscription, 'Annual parliaments—universal suffrage—vote by ballot—no property qualification—payment of members—our cause is just.' Beside it was a plain pink flag. A band of music here was stationed. Next came a number of small flags borne by children, and then a large green flag, with the inscription, 'Feargus O'Connor, the Friend of Equal Rights and Equal Laws.' Two small flags, green and pink, with 'Feargus O'Connor' on them. A number of small flags came next, and then likenesses of Oastler, O'Connor, and Emmet framed into a triangular shape, and mounted on the tops of poles, presented a gay appearance : surmounting them were caps of liberty, made of crimson satin, and embroidered imitation pearls. Next came another band of music, and behind it the carriage and four greys, containing O'Connor standing up, with Dean Taylor, and other friends of the Chartist cause beside him. Mr. Sweet occupied the box. A number of flags and flys drawn by single horses, full of women and men, followed. Next came a large banner with the boot-makers' arms on it—a very valuable and choice flag. The next flag bore the inscription, 'They have set up Kings, but not by me—God is our King—him will I obey.' A next flag bore the inscription, 'We have set our lives upon the cast, and we will stand the hazard of the die'. A band of music followed—we learnt it was the Sutton Forest Band. A large green flag was next conspicuous, with the inscription, 'The Carrington Chartists, in Honor of Feargus O'Connor'. A number of small flags, and phaetons drawn by single horses, loaded 'above a bit'. A large red flag, having on it 'Freedom to the whole Family of Man,'—a pink flag, 'Union is Strength'—a green flag with 'The Charter,' on one side, and 'No Surrender,' on the other—a large flag with 'Ilkeston National Association'— a white flag with 'No Surrender' upon it, and the Heanor band closed the procession.

In Nottingham market-place O'Connor delivered a characteristic harangue. He afterwards claimed that forty thousand people heard him. 'Such a demonstration yesterday,' he wrote to the *Northern Star*, 'as Nottingham never before witnessed.'[12]

In the months after O'Connor's release from prison trade depression reached its peak. This helped to intensify the welcome

12. *Nottingham Review*, Feb. 25; *Northern Star*, Feb. 26, March 5, 1842.

given to O'Connor on his tours through the industrial districts. Backed by widespread distress Chartism moved towards another climax. It went through the same motions as in 1839, although the events of that year had proved their futility. Another National Convention met on April 12, 1842; a second National Petition was prepared. This described once again the sufferings and grievances of the people and demanded enactment of the six points of the Charter. It also demanded repeal of the Union with Ireland.

Apart from arranging the presentation of the petition, the National Convention had little to do. It spent its time in vague discussion and bickering. An unconvincing reconciliation was arranged between O'Connor and O'Brien, who respectively proposed and seconded a motion urging all Chartists to avoid quarrelling.[13]

On May 2nd the Chartist petition was presented in the Commons by T. S. Duncombe, Radical member for Finchley. It had been carried in procession two miles long through London, O'Connor marching at the head of the Convention delegates. It was taken into the houses of parliament by forty or fifty men, O'Connor himself carrying a bundle. The Chartists claimed that it had 3,315,752 signatures, over two-and-a-half times the number of the 1839 petition. Duncombe listed the localities where it had received most support. Lancashire and Cheshire towns contributed three hundred thousand signatures, London and its suburbs two hundred thousand, the West Riding over a hundred and seventy thousand, Newcastle and district ninety-two thousand, Glasgow and Larnarkshire seventy-eight thousand, Nottingham forty thousand.

The following day the Commons discussed the petition. Duncombe was supported in the debate by other Radicals, opposed by Macaulay, who contended that universal suffrage would be fatal to the constitution. J. A. Roebuck spoke in favour of Chartist principles but dissociated himself from the Chartist leaders. He described O'Connor, although not naming him, as a 'malignant and cowardly demagogue.' Roebuck's speech gave the Whig and Tory leaders an easy excuse to dispose of the petition. Lord John Russell pointed out that if universal suffrage were conceded O'Connor would certainly be elected to parliament; his character

---

13. *Northern Star,* April 23, 30, 1842.

being as Roebuck asserted, would there not then be danger of spoliation of property? If they heard the petitioners at the bar, asked Peel, the Prime Minister, who would be their spokesman?—the cowardly, malignant demagogue O'Connor. Only forty-nine members voted for Duncombe, two hundred and eighty-seven against. O'Connor, who was in the gallery, had heard it generally assumed that his connection with National Petition was sufficient reason for rejecting it. He challenged Roebuck to a duel, which, according to Feargus, he only avoided by completely disavowing the obvious application of his remarks.[14]

Once again parliament had been unimpressed by the noise made by the Chartists and their leader. As in 1839, elation was followed by deflation. But at least this time O'Connor seems to have begun to learn the lesson of Chartist failure before parliament. Feargus now saw that the Chartists must be much stronger in the country before they approached parliament again. Noise and number alone were not enough : they must have economic weight. 'Our Charter must be carried out of the House before it is even temperately discussed in the House,' he remarked in the *Northern Star* on May 7th. He saw two ways in which the working-classes might gain economic weight : either by adopting a plan for settlement in large numbers upon the land and thereby building up their independence, or by an alliance with the propertied middle-classes. A land scheme had been in his mind for years, but after the failure of the 1842 petition he turned first to the idea of a middle-class alliance.

Hitherto he had revelled in denunciations of the middle-classes. They were the employers who ground the people down, who alone had benefited from the Reform Act, who opposed the Ten Hours Bill and who supported the New Poor Law, and who had founded the Anti-Corn Law League in order to get cheap bread and lower wages. The *Northern Star* had once described class conflict as part of the law of nature.[15]

---

14. *Parliamentary Debates*, third series, LXII (1842), 1373-81; LXIII (1842), 13-91; *Northern Star*, May 7, 1842; *National Instructor*, 312; R. E. Leader, *Life and Letters of John Arthur Roebuck* (1897), 143, 195-96.

15. See A. Briggs, 'Chartism Reconsidered', in *Historical Studies, Papers read before the Third Conference of Irish Historians* (ed. M. Roberts, 1959), 52-54; Briggs (ed.), *Chartist Studies*, 295-97.

We have seen how in January 1841 O'Connor had brought about the defeat in Leeds of an attempt to unite middle- and working-class reformers. At the end of the year the middle-class Radicals repeated the attempt upon a national scale. Certain members of the Anti-Corn Law League, led by Joseph Sturge, a Birmingham Quaker, formed the Complete Suffrage Union. As a Christian, Sturge was disturbed by the class cleavage and conflict within the new industrial society. He decided that the equality of men must be acknowledged by giving the working-classes the vote. On April 5, 1842 a Complete Suffrage conference opened at Birmingham. Lovett, O'Brien and other Chartists attended. The meeting agreed to adopt the principles of the Charter, although the middle-class reformers refused to accept the Chartist label and solution of this important difficulty had to be left over. All this was before the rejection of the National Petition, while O'Connor was still implacably hostile to the middle-classes. He denounced the conference as another middle-class trick to draw the people away from their own movement into the selfish Anti-Corn Law League. He dubbed Sturge's movement 'Complete Humbug'; and to emphasise his hostility he called a public meeting in Birmingham for the opening day of the conference. In his speech at this meeting he strongly attacked Sturge.[16]

But after the failure of the National Petition O'Connor completely reversed his attitude to the Complete Suffrage movement. He had at last realised—the realisation at this time was to be only temporary—that in the economic, social and political circumstances of the 1840s the working-classes could not achieve reform without middle-class assistance. From June 15th to August 13th he published in the *Northern Star* a series of letters 'to the Industrious Portion of the Middling Classes'. He Argued that their distress was as great as that of the operatives, that the existing system protected them no better than it protected the people, and that only through universal suffrage could it be reformed. If given the vote, the people would not threaten property and capital but would defend it since they would now have a stake in the community. O'Connor called for a union of classes to achieve the Charter under the Chartist name, 'hallowed by persecution, and rendered dear by oppression and opposition.' He tried to

16. *Northern Star*, March 26, April 2, 9, 1842.

overcome middle-class dislike of him personally : 'Suppose that I was the very worst of men; would that furnish a justifiable excuse for withholding your support for the very best of principles?'

O'Connor soon began to think that he was making progress in winning middle-class support. He pointed joyfully to a meeting of distressed shopkeepers in Burnley which had asked the government to adopt the Charter. 'What force can now affright us?' asked Feargus. 'What force can now vanquish us? ... You are now more powerful than the whole Corn Law League.'[17]

At the beginning of August 1842 Sturge stood at a bye-election in Nottingham. At the Chartist meeting there in the previous February O'Connor had denounced Sturge as a middle-class trickster. Now he went to Nottingham to lead the local Chartists in support of Sturge. Thomas Cooper came over from Leicester to assist his idol. J. R. Stephens, who since his imprisonment had lapsed into his own brand of Toryism, came to support John Walter, the Tory candidate. At a meeting on the night before the election one of the most notable of all British election fights broke out between O'Connor's men and those of Stephens. The Nottingham 'lambs,' notorious for their violence and intimidation at elections, had been engaged on the Tory side; but on this occasion they were overcome by O'Connor's Chartists. For three-quarters of an hour the Chartists refused to give the renegade Stephens a hearing, tearing up in his face copies of his portrait which had been given away with the *Northern Star* in 1838 when he was a Chartist hero. Eventually, according to the Chartist version, the Tory 'lambs' charged the reformers' waggon. The peace-loving Sturge retired, but O'Connor and his Chartists defended themselves. At first the surprise attack drove them back, but at the right moment Feargus called upon his men to counter-charge, himself jumping down from the waggon to lead his followers. Like a true Irishman O'Connor revelled in the mêlée.' According to Thomas Cooper, he floored the Tory 'lambs' like nine-pins. Once he was himself knocked down, but his red head soon bobbed up again. Gradually the 'lambs' were forced back to the Tory waggon. O'Connor sprang at it, parrying a kick at his head and to the cheers of the people bringing the kicker down head first. Finally the Tory waggon was taken and overturned. O'Connor,

17. *Northern Star,* July 23, 1842.

Cooper and others then addressed the meeting uninterrupted.

The next day, August 4th, was polling day. Hopes were high for Sturge; but Tory bribery just defeated him, Walter winning by eighty-four votes.[18]

A few days after the Nottingham bye-election the Plug Strikes broke out. They were given this name because in the factory districts operatives went round pulling plugs out of mill boilers to prevent work. The Plug Strikes were a spontaneous movement of protest against unemployment, low wages and distress. Lancashire was the centre, but the outbreak spread throughout the manufacturing districts, involving cotton and woollen factory workers and handloom weavers, colliers, pottery workers and many more. The Chartists did not organise the strikes. In fact, the movement indicated a decline in Chartist influence following the failure of the National Petition: the people had turned from political to economic action. The Chartists attributed the strikes to the Anti-Corn Law League. They claimed that the League manufacturers had deliberately provoked the cotton operatives to strike by making excessive wage reductions in the hope that the resulting confusion would force the government to concede repeal of the Corn Laws. The government itself strongly suspected the League of organising the outbreak. During the previous months Cobden and Bright had certainly been contemplating extreme measures. A general refusal by League members to pay taxes and a mass lock-out were both considered by them and rejected only on practical not on moral or legal grounds. But the League does not seem to have played a deliberate part in provoking the outbreak, although the intemperate language used by its speakers during the previous months undoubtedly added to the atmosphere of tension out of which the strikes came.

O'Connor and the *Northern Star*, however, consistently treated the Plug Strikes as a League conspiracy. In the *Star* of August 20th O'Connor published further details (he had first written of the matter in the number for July 16th) of a conversation which he claimed to have had at Halifax on July 6th with Acland, a League lecturer. O'Connor claimed that Acland had admitted that the League was planning an outbreak. Acland hotly denied

---

18. Ibid, May 14, Aug. 6; *Nottingham Review*, Feb. 25, Aug. 5, 1842; Cooper, *Life*, 156-61.

this in the *Morning Chronicle* and in the *Anti-Bread-Tax Circular*, the League organ. According to Acland, O'Connor had asked, 'Will the League stop all the mills?' Acland had replied, 'That would give you the *Charter* in three weeks, which you can hardly expect from long-headed men who are no Chartists.' O'Connor then remarked that the middle-classes had no other practical means of obtaining Corn Law repeal, to which Acland answered that non-payment of taxes would achieve it in three months.[19]

Whatever its origins, how were the Chartists to react to the Plug Strikes? Many of the strikers voted at their meetings for the Charter, although the cry for 'a fair day's wage for a fair day's work' was much louder. By a concidence, a Chartist national delegate meeting had been called to meet in Manchester on August 17th. On the previous day, the anniversary of Peterloo, O'Connor was to unveil a memorial to Henry Hunt, the chief speaker at the massacre. The Chartist conference resolved to call upon the strikers to remain out until the Charter became the law of the land. Hill, however, editor of the *Northern Star*, spoke against supporting the movement, arguing that the strikes were a League trick which would only spread misery among the people and would not advance the Charter. These were probably O'Connor's views also; but finding a large majority of the delegates in favour of the strike, Feargus, anxious not to damage his popularity, voted with them. M'Douall, a Chartist extremist, next drew up a fiercely worded manifesto threatening violence in support of the strike and of the Charter, and urging the people to leave the decision to the god of battles. M'Douall wanted this also to be sent out in the name of the conference. Hill protested strongly against it. O'Connor proposed that it be published in the name of the executive of the N.C.A. only, and this was done. O'Connor was not a member of the executive and so did not sign the threatening document. This may have been the reason for his proposal. In the event, however, his close connection with the manifesto led to his prosecution alongside its signatories.[20]

Immediately after the appearance of the manifesto on placards

19. *Northern Star*, July 16, Aug. 20; *Anti-Bread-Tax Circular*, Aug. 25, 1842; *Trial of Feargus O'Connor and Fifty-Eight Others at Lancaster* (1843), 399-439.
20. *Northern Star*, Aug. 20, 27, Sept. 3, 1842; Cooper, *Life*, 207-11.

in Manchester large-scale arrests of Chartist leaders began. The
government had been waiting to act at the first opportunity.
O'Connor now began bitterly to regret that he had not insisted
upon a more moderate line at the conference. He denounced
M'Douall in the *Northern Star* of August 27th for 'breathing a
wild strain of recklessness most dangerous to the cause'. Once
again O'Connor's correspondence was opened by the authorities.[21]

Yet whatever policy the Chartists had followed, whether they
had threatened or even used violence in support of the strikes, or
whether they had been more temperate, or had they stood
completely aside, the strike movement was bound to fail. The
people were not sufficiently organised to hold out for long. Gradually, those who had work to go to drifted back to it without any
increase in wages. The strike had not helped them. Nor had it
helped the Chartist leaders, whose maladroit attempt to exploit
it had led them into the courts.

O'Connor and Hill were among the last Chartist leaders to be
arrested, not until the end of September. Sir James Graham, the
Home Secretary, had been hoping to indict them for high treason;
but the Law Officers eventually decided that there was not sufficient evidence to support such a charge and O'Connor was finally
indicted for seditious conspiracy. Fifty-nine men, Chartist and
trade union leaders, were charged together :

> I propose to charge O'Connor as a general conspirator with
> the others, wrote Sir Frederick Pollock, the Attorney-General,
> to Graham, 'and not to proceed against him for Libel merely,
> or for acting as a Delegate, or taking part at the meeting of
> Delegates—I propose to try him in the same indictment with
> the worst of the defendants who headed mobs, made seditious
> speeches, and stopped mills and factories. I shall blend in one
> accusation the head and the hands—the bludgeon and the
> pen, and let the jury and the public see in one case the whole
> crime, its commencement and its consequences.

To underline the gravity of the Chartists' offences Pollock
suggested that the case be transferred to Westminster for trial at
Bar before the full Court of Queen's Bench. This suggestion was
at first favourably considered by the government but was ulti-

---

21. Mather, *Public Order in the Age of the Chartists*, 221.

mately not taken up since the transfer would probably have been contested in court, causing delay and thereby destroying the atmosphere of urgency which it was desired to create. The trial did not come on at Lancaster until March 1843.[22]

O'Connor sincerely believed that the Anti-Corn Law League had instigated the Plug Strikes. He was furious that he and his fellow Chartists, not Cobden, Acland and the League leaders, had been prosecuted as a result of the outbreak. The Chartists had been made the 'scrapegoat' for the League.[23] This feeling of injustice led O'Connor completely to abandon his recent friendly policy towards the Complete Suffrage party, whose leaders were also prominent members of the League. A Complete Suffrage conference was called for Birmingham on December 27, 1842. After the Plug Strikes O'Connor decided to smash this conference. 'Here then we may try our strength against Whiggery, and if elected, there I will go to lend my hand in its destruction. No man in his senses can fail to see what is now going on, and the leaning of the Complete Suffragites to the Free Trade party.' The Chartists secured a majority among the delegates elected to attend the conference. To the alarm of Sturge, O'Connor himself was chosen to represent Birmingham, Sturge's own stronghold. When the conference met the Sturgeites still tried to avoid adopting the Chartist label, proposing instead a 'Bill of Rights' including the six points. By doing so they played into O'Connor's hands, who now wished to break off all negotiations with them. O'Connor and Lovett came into unexpected alliance. Lovett denounced the Sturge bill, O'Connor seconded him. A bitter debate followed. Lovett's resolution was carried by more than two to one, and the Sturgeites thereupon withdrew from the conference. The Complete Suffrage movement was dead as a significant political force. The Chartist-middle-class alliance had come to nothing.[24]

The trial of O'Connor and fifty-eight others opened at Lan-

---

22. Briggs (ed.), *Chartist Studies,* 391-93.
23. *Trial of Feargus O'Connor,* 291; *Parliamentary Debates,* third series, CIX (1850), 172.
24. *Northern Star,* Dec. 10-31, 1842; Cooper, *Life,* 221-28.
25. The fullest account is *The Trial of Feargus O'Connor and Fifty-Eight Others at Lancaster* (1843), with a commentary by F. O'Connor.

caster on March 1, 1843.[25] The judge was Baron Rolfe; the Attorney-General led for the Crown; O'Connor defended himself. He conducted his defence much more successfully than at his trial in 1840, when the case against him had hardly been disputable. This time he had much more ground for manoeuvre. He was especially effective in discrediting the two principal witnesses for the Crown. On the eighth day of the trial the judge summed up, in terms more favourable to the Chartists than had been expected. O'Connor and fourteen others were found guilty only on the fifth of nine counts in the indictment, that of endeavouring to excite disaffection by unlawfully encouraging a stoppage of labour. Sixteen defendants were found guilty on the more serious fourth count of using threats and encouraging tumult to produce a stoppage of labour.

The Attorney-General was much disappointed by the outcome of the trial. He thought that the judge had 'totally lost sight of the great features of the case,' which the monster indictment had been intended to bring out. He concluded that Rolfe was tired and ill, an influenza epidemic prevailing during the trial, which took place against a background of coughs and sneezes.[26]

In the event even the limited decision against the Chartists was not upheld. Counsel for the prisoners sued for a writ of error on the ground of incorrect wording of the indictment. The prisoners were liberated while the point was considered, and they were never afterwards called up for sentence. Feargus O'Connor was left free to lead the Chartist movement in a new direction.

---

26. *Personal Remembrances of Sir Frederick Pollock* (1887), I, 204-5.

CHAPTER XI

THE LAND PLAN

AFTER the failure of the second National Petition in May 1842 Feargus O'Connor had weighed in his mind two lines of future action. First, he had tried for union with the middle-classes. But after the Plug Strikes he had turned angrily away from this policy, and he now turned to his second idea, the Land Plan.

Like much else in O'Connor's career some of the inspiration for the Land Plan came from his uncle, Arthur O'Connor. In his pamphlet, *State of Ireland,* published in 1798, Arthur O'Connor had advocated a system of small farms. Significantly, in 1843 at the beginning of his Land Plan campaign Feargus republished this pamphlet, adding an introduction by himself. He contended that his uncle had proved that no country could be prosperous or her people independent without a small farm system and without universal suffrage.

Feargus O'Connor's views on the land question were probably also influenced by William Cobbett, who had advocated 'spade culture' in his *Political Register* in 1827. Instead of using the plough, a piece of machinery which displaced human labour, Cobbett had urged the exclusive use of the spade. 'Everything,' he wrote, 'that can be done by wheels, by iron, by steel, by wood, by horses, has been done by them, as it were for the purpose of starving the labouring classes out of existence.' As early as 1830 Feargus outlined a small allotment plan, based upon spade culture, to O'Neill Daunt, his neighbour in Co. Cork. In 1848 he told parliament that he had tried out his system with a hundred and thirty labourers upon part of his Cork estate.[1]

---

1. G. D. H. Cole, *Life of William Cobbett* (3rd ed., 1947), 311-12; W. J. O'Neill Daunt, *Personal Recollections of the late Daniel O'Connell* (1848), I, 50; *Parliamentary Debates,* third series, XCVII (1848), 694.

O'Connor's enthusiasm for the Land Plan thus antedated his attachment to the Chartist movement. He first conceived it as a plan to overcome the misery of the Irish peasants. After he became a Chartist O'Connor sought to apply it also to overcome the sufferings of the English industrial operatives. The Land Plan was to be a main part of the programme of the Anglo-Irish working-class alliance for which O'Connor always pressed.

At the beginning of 1843 the *Northern Star* began a persistent campaign to interest the Chartists in the land.[2] On February 11th a long article appeared describing new machinery about to be introduced in the woollen industry. 'It is our purpose that the working man shall be fairly forewarned of what is in immediate preparation for him.' Woollen manufacture was about to be transformed : if the operatives were unprepared they would be overwhelmed. They must be ready to return to the land. Surplus operatives settled on smallholdings would prosper as they could never hope to do in industry; and after surplus labour had been drained off, those still left in industry would be able to demand fair wages and better conditions. Only in these circumstances could machinery reduce the toil of industrial life without depriving many operatives of work altogether; only in this way could it become (in a favourite phrase of O'Connor's) 'man's holiday' instead of 'man's curse.'

This machinery argument was a main part of O'Connor's case for the Land Plan. Another argument stressed the social and moral benefits of a smallholder system. By returning to the land operatives would regain the independence which they had lost under the industrial system. They would be free from employers. O'Connor put this point strongly :

You are, in a word, a poor, beggarly, lousy set of devils! Without house or home, or bread, or clothes, or fuel; begging

---

2. Except where otherwise indicated, the account of the Land Plan which follows is based upon the six reports of the select committee of inquiry into the National Land Company *Accounts & Papers*, xix (398), (420), (451), (503), (559), (577), 1847-48; upon Joy MacAskill, 'The Chartist Land Plan' in Briggs (ed.), *Chartist Studies;* and upon W. H. G. Armytage, 'The Chartist Land Colonies 1846-1848', *Agricultural History*, vol. 32 (1958).

the means of subsistence, and thankful to him who will coin
your sweat into gold! . . .
    Now mark what you might be! Just what you have made
others, comfortable, independent, and happy! thanking no
man for the means of subsistence!

The Land Plan, in other words, was a way of escape from the
suffering and servitude of the new industrial society.

The passage just quoted came in a series of letters from O'Connor
'To the Producers of Wealth, and all those who live by Industry
on the Land', which appeared in the *Northern Star* from April
15 to May 27, 1843. In these letters O'Connor outlined a detailed
plan of land settlement. He proposed that five thousand heads
of families from industrial towns should be settled on twenty
thousand acres of land, four acres per family, on some forty estates
throughout the country. Each estate was to have its own community centre, schools, library and hospital. By spade husbandry
O'Connor was confident that the smallholders would quickly
prosper, that they would soon be able to produce ample quantities
of root crops for their subsistence and for the market. He promised
to organise and finance the scheme within a year. Once the people
had seen the success of these model establishments they would want
the government to establish land settlements upon a national scale.
The government would not do this until universal suffrage was
achieved : the achievement of the Land Plan and of the Charter
thus went together, they were '*Siamese twins*'.

    In the summer of 1843 O'Connor published in parts a book
called *A Practical Work on the Management of Small Farms*
which elaborated his plan. It gave glowing accounts of his own
success as an agriculturalist in Ireland and offered detailed advice
on the cultivation of certain crops.

    O'Connor's Land Plan was not a socialist venture like Owen's
contemporary colony at Queenwood. O'Connor's Irish background
made him prefer a system of independent proprietorship and
cultivation. He wanted co-operation but not communal living or
common ownership.

    'Communism', he wrote in *The Labourer* in 1847, 'either
destroys wholesome emulation and competition, or else it
fixes too high a price upon distinction, and must eventually
end in the worst description of despotism—the despotism of

self-surrender and non-reliance on self; whilst, upon the other hand individual possession and co-operation of labour creates a wholesome bond between all classes of society, which none can push beyond the will or requirement of his neighbour.'[3]

At a conference of the National Charter Association at Birmingham in September 1843 O'Connor's Land Plan was approved in principle. He now joined the executive of the N.C.A.[4] After the conference, however, no progress was made in implementing the scheme. Another Chartist delegate meeting at Manchester in April 1844 did not even notice the land question. Trade was now flourishing, and Chartism had lost much of its support. In July 1844 O'Connor could claim no more than that 'Chartism is not dead but sleeping.'[5]

At a national delegate meeting in London in April 1845 Feargus was at last able to get his plan under way. The conference agreed to found a Chartist Co-Operative Land Society, with O'Connor in virtually complete control of its affairs. The society proposed to buy good arable land at £18 15s. an acre. If £5,000 were raised, this would buy a hundred and twenty acres, giving sixty heads of families two acres each and leaving a balance of £2,750 for cottages, stock, &c. These allotments might be leased in perpetuity to members at £5 annual rent. The gross annual rental would thus be £300. If sold at twenty years' purchase the property would thus fetch £6,000. This sum, expended in the same manner, would place seventy-two heads of families upon the land. These seventy-two allotments sold at the rate of the first would bring in £7,200. This money could be used to locate eighty-six heads of families. And so the snowball would go on. In a few years all the surplus industrial population could be placed upon the land.[6]

It will be seen that, unlike the scheme of 1843, this plan was self-developing. Government help was no longer envisaged. The Land Plan could now be effected before the Charter was achieved. Once the people were independent upon the land they would

---

3. *The Labourer*, I, 149; *Northern Star*, April 15, 1843.
4. *Northern Star*, Sept. 9, 1843.
5. Ibid, July 27, 1844.
6. Ibid, April 26, May 3, 1845.

be in a much stronger position to carry the Charter. Here was an important shift in emphasis. For the rest of his political career achievement of the Land Plan took precedence in O'Connor's mind over achievement of the Charter.

Shares were to be issued by the new Land Company to raise the initial capital of £5,000. Each share was to cost £2 10s., but they could be bought by weekly subscriptions of 3d. upwards. Tenants for the estates were to be chosen by ballot from among shareholders. At the end of 1846 a Chartist Land Bank was launched as another means of collecting capital. Savings of members invested in the bank were to be applied to the redemption of their rent charge when they became occupants. 'If those with money would lend it,' wrote O'Connor in May 1847, 'at three-and-a-half per cent., on the best security in the world, I would change the whole face of society in TWELVE MONTHS from this day ... I would make a paradise of England in less than FIVE YEARS.'[7]

O'Connor tried to register the Land Company under the Friendly Societies Act; but the registrar refused to accept this on the ground that the company was a political body. O'Connor then provisionally registered the company under the Joint Stock Companies Act. But he found that complete registration would be very expensive. To circumvent this he moved in March 1848 to introduce a bill in the Commons bringing the Land Company under the Friendly Societies Act. This bill, however, was never given a second reading. The Land Company was never fully registered; and the Commons, instead of passing O'Connor's bill, appointed a select committee to inquire into the whole position of the Land Company.

These legal difficulties did not at first depress O'Connor. He believed intensely in his plan. He lived completely for it, going about as Ernest Jones later recalled, in a 'state of joyous excitement'. 'It will be the proudest day of my life,' exclaimed Feargus in 1845, 'when I see the first batch of colonists entering their "own castles".' O'Connor loved the Land Plan the more because it was his own, both in conception and in execution. The Anti-Poor Law and Chartist movements had been begun by others, although he had forced his leadership upon them both. Feargus had virtu-

---

7. *Northern Star*, May 8, 1847.

ally a free hand in running the Land Company. Its officers were all his protégés. Lovett, O'Brien and others opposed the Land Plan as impracticable, but O'Connor had by now almost driven them out of the Chartist movement.[8]

After the conference of April 1845 Feargus toured the country viewing estates and publicising his plan. By December, when the first Chartist conference devoted exclusively to the Land Plan was held, thirty districts had been organised for the collection of funds. This conference was held at Manchester, Lancashire being the earliest strong centre of support for the Land Plan. Support extended and intensified after the purchase for £2,344 of the first estate, Heronsgate near Watford, in March 1846. This estate was renamed O'Connorville. Its ceremonial inauguration took place on August 17, 1846, Chartists attending from all parts of the country. A procession of vehicles left Hyde Park Corner at 7 a.m., arriving at the site at mid-day. Refreshment booths were provided and a booth for dancing. Ernest Jones, a rising young protégé of O'Connor, wrote a poem for the occasion which was widely publicised. In the afternoon O'Connor and Jones addressed the crowds. O'Connor's tone was bouyant :[9]

> He stood there rejoicing in being the best abused man, not in England, but in the world . . . He was called a leveller, but he laughed the name to scorn; he was an elevator . . . He required new land marks for a new population as he required new books for new minds. Fences nine yards wide, occupying over six acres of this farm, were the old land marks; a post and a rail would be the new land marks. (Cheers.) An old farm house built of lath and plaster, and tiles, was the old land mark; the labourer's cottage built of brick, of the best brick, stuccoed outside, and with gutters, were the new land marks. (Loud cheers).

On May Day 1847 the settlers moved into O'Connorville. The estate of about a hundred acres was divided into two, three and four acre plots intersected by paths which were called Bradford Road, Halifax Road, Stockport Road and Nottingham Road. A school house had been built. The intention may have been to

8. Ibid, May 31, 1845; *People's Paper,* April 16, 1853.
9. *Northern Star,* Aug. 22, 1846.

run the estate on temperance principles, but a public house called 'The Land of Liberty' (which still stands) was soon opened nearby. On the opening day of the estate O'Connor delivered another exultant speech :

> What I now witness is but a feeble outline—a meagre unfinished sketch of that full-length portrait of freedom, happiness, and contentment which will eventually result from the novelty I have ventured to propound. (Cheers.) While joy fills your hearts here, the song of gladness resounds throughout the land. (Loud cheers.)

At one point Feargus broke down in tears at the prospect which he saw of the transformation of the condition of the people through the Land Plan.[10]

In August 1847 a second estate at Lowbands in Gloucestershire was opened and in June 1848 a third at Snig's End a few miles away. Two more estates were planned, but never settled, in the West Midlands. An estate renamed Charterville, near Witney in Oxfordshire, was opened on a bleak unsuitable site in March 1848. Most of the settlers on these estates came from the manufacturing districts. Some were factory operatives, but craftsmen (tailors, shoemakers, &c.) were also prominent. Few of the most distressed operatives, handloom weavers or framework knitters, seem to have become settlers, no doubt because they were too poor to buy shares in the company.

Over £100,000 was subscribed in all by about seventy thousand members of the Land Company. Yet by the middle of 1848 only about two hundred and fifty operatives had been settled in allotments. Progress was thus pathetically slow in proportion to the money subscribed. Moreover, of the estates established only O'Connerville at all prospered. It was not as easy as O'Connor had claimed for town workmen to earn a living by spade husbandry off small plots of land. As the *Edinburgh Review* remarked :[11]

> Every estimate seemed to be made on the supposition of a perpetual miraculous interposition ... Every acre was to yield on an *average* such crops as no acre ever did yield except

---

10. *Northern Star,* May 8, 1847.
11. *Edinburgh Review,* XLV (1852), 432.

under the rarest combinations of favouring climate, consummate skill, and unlimited manure—and then only occasionally. Every cow was to live for ever, was to give more milk than any save the most exceptional kine ever gave before, and was never to be dry. Every pig was to be a prize one—every goose to be a swan.

None of the estates reached the stage where they might profitably be mortgaged, for the tenants could not pay their rents. In any case, the mortgage plan would not have worked. As O'Brien pointed out, if the plan had begun to succeed on any large scale the effect would have been to raise the price of land, thereby undermining the whole mortgage position.[12]

As it got under way the Land Plan had to face strong criticism from certain middle-class newspapers. The *Nottingham Journal* and the *Nottingham Mercury* were especially persistent, O'Connor having been elected to parliament for Nottingham in 1847. The *Mercury* denounced the Land Plan as 'a vulgar combination of autocratism, helotism, and Irishism.' It stressed how much the plan was Irish in conception; O'Connor's ideal was possession of a pig-sty and a potato-plot. 'He has no idea of a working man or his family rising in the world—pushing their fortunes, or extending the sphere of their enjoyments. His wish seems to be to entail poverty.'[13]

In February 1850 O'Connor sued Job Bradshaw, proprietor of the *Nottingham Journal,* for libel. The *Journal* had sarcastically invited subscriptions for the Land Company from admirers of O'Connor, 'who has wheedled the people of England out of £100,000, with which he bought estates and conveyed them to his own use and benefit.' All who wished to witness the overthrow of 'this great political imposter' were invited to order the *Journal* wherein he would be exposed. At his trial Bradshaw was defended by J. A. Roebuck, who had expressed his dislike of O'Connor in the Commons in 1842. Roebuck pointed out, as many critics had done, that O'Connor had bought the estates in his own name, and Bradshaw was acquitted. A rider to the verdict stated that O'Connor stood 'unimpeached as regards his personal honesty,'

---

12. Gammage, *Chartist Movement*, 268-69.
13. *Nottingham Mercury*, Aug. 13—Oct. 22, 1847.

but this was poor compensation for the heavy legal costs which he had to bear.[14]

O'Connor had been forced to buy land in his own name because the position of the Land Company had never been fully legalised. This illegality was made clear in the six reports of the select committee of the Commons which appeared in the summer of 1848. The committee also found that the finances of the Land Company were in confusion. The committee did not accuse O'Connor of deliberate dishonesty; it noted that he had sunk over £3,000 of his own money in the company. But its reports shattered confidence in him as a businessman. After August 1848 subscriptions to the Land Company slumped suddenly. The bubble had burst.

Yet for two years more O'Connor still continued to hope that his plan might be saved. As late as August 3, 1850 he was announcing in the *Northern Star* that he intended to embark upon a speaking tour to 'resuscitate the Chartist movement, and propound the means by which every industrious man shall be emancipated from the rasp of the blood-sucker, by the application of free labour to the cultivation of HIS OWN LAND.' In August 1851 the Land Company was formally dissolved by special act of parliament.

O'Connor had set all his hopes upon the Land Plan. Its failure, preceded in April 1848 by the failure of the Kennington Common meeting, gradually sent him mad. His letters in the *Northern Star* attacking critics of the plan became more and more unbalanced. His speeches, never logical, grew increasingly incoherent.

Very little was saved from the wreck of the Land Plan. At Charterville only two of the original settlers seem to have been still in possession of their plots at the time of the census of 1851; at O'Connorville there were then six survivors, at Lowbands sixteen and at Snig's End twenty-two. O'Connor, desperate for money to meet the costs of the Bradshaw case, was himself indirectly responsible for evicting most of the Charterville tenants for non-payment of rent. The *Oxford Chronicle* described their departure in November 1850. Many of them were penniless, 'and exclaimed loudly against the scheme, which in the first instance, told such a plausible tale of the lasting benefits it would confer on

---

14. *Nottingham Journal*, Feb. 22, Nov. 22, 1850.

the shareholders, but which now had reduced them to the necessity of returning from whence they came.'[15]

The great vision thus disintegrated, and its projector himself disintegrated with it. Proof at least of how deeply and sincerely Feargus O'Connor was attached to his Land Plan.

15. *Oxford Chronicle*, Nov. 23, 1850, quoted Briggs (ed.), *Chartist Studies*, 333.

CHAPTER XII

REPEAL OF THE CORN LAWS

THE Chartist movement had as its contemporary the middle-class Anti-Corn Law League, founded early in 1839. The often violent rivalry between the two movements added to the tensions of the time. We have already seen how the League organised the local Irish to break up Chartist meetings in Manchester. But the Chartists had begun the game. From the start of the League agitation the Chartists had intruded at its meetings both in Manchester, the League headquarters, and throughout the industrial districts. Perhaps their most striking intervention was at a meeting in the Manchester Corn Exchange on February 28, 1839. Delegates were to report back at this meeting from an anti-Corn Law conference in London. The Manchester Chartists attended in force and proposed one 'honest Pat Murphy,' a potato-wheeler, for the chair. The Leaguers refused to accept him, and thereupon the Chartists broke up the meeting. The League was forced to hold it again a week later with admission by ticket only.[1]

The Anti-Corn Law League was compelled to take on a predominantly middle-class character; but its leaders always aspired to attract working-class support. Before the establishment of the League the chief argument against the Corn Laws had been a cheap labour one, that lower corn prices would enable manufacturers to reduce wages, thereby increasing the competitive power of British industry abroad and also (although this point was not paraded) increasing the profits of manufacture. This cheap labour argument, although attractive to manufacturers, offered few benefits from Corn Law repeal for their operatives. Richard Cob-

---

1. A Prentice, *History of the Anti-Corn Law League* (1853), I, 116-20.

den, the leader of the Anti-Corn Law League, replaced it with a variety of new arguments designed to appeal to working men. Prominent among these was the cumulative prosperity argument. This claimed that unrestricted importation of foreign corn must encourage foreign buying of our manufactures by way of return, thereby increasing production and the demand for labour and consequently increasing wages.

Whether many of the manufacturers who supported the Anti-Corn Law League had really given up the selfish cheap labour motive is doubtful. The Chartists refused to believe it. They regarded the League simply as an organisation seeking means to extort still more profit out of the labour of working men. This was the chief reason for Chartist intervention at League meetings.

Yet some Chartist leaders were prepared to accept repeal of the Corn Laws after the Charter had been achieved. Other Chartists, by contrast, were complete protectionists. At different times Feargus O'Connor put forward both points of view; but on the whole he seems to have favoured repeal after achievement of the Charter. In the *Northern Star* in 1838 he admitted that as an Irish member of parliament he had opposed repeal. He had then represented an agricultural county, and the Corn Laws were in the interests of landlords. But he had changed his mind when he found that those landlords, despite the protection of the Corn Law, refused to reduce rents to a fair level. He wrote that he now supported repeal because the industrial operatives needed cheap bread; but he emphasised that they could only ensure that they got cheap bread without cheap wages by securing the Charter.[2]

O'Connor thus believed that government protection would be needed to ensure the benefits of Corn Law repeal for the operatives. He was unimpressed by Cobden's cumulative prosperity argument, which promised cheap bread and high wages without government intervention. 'Well but trade would increase! So it would, and prodigiously, for a while, until by a corresponding increase of machinery, the masters could place themselves to do the thing in the cheapest way.'[3]

Up to 1844 O'Connor regarded Richard Cobden, the League leader, as a typical representative of the grasping manufacturers.

---

2. *Northern Star*, March 24, Sept. 1, 1838.
3. Ibid, Aug. 7, 1841; *Trial of Feargus O'Connor*, v.

In a series of open letters addressed to Cobden early in that year Feargus jeered at 'the glib philosophy and sophistry of mountebank cosmopolites, who would hang this vast world upon a Free Trade peg.'[4] Several times O'Connor challenged Cobden to public debate upon the Corn Laws. They met at last on August 5, 1844 at Northampton. Cobden made a typical reasoned speech; O'Connor replied with an equally typical effusion, touching on many points but weak in overall argument. Taken by itself it was no worse than many of his speeches, but as an answer to Cobden it was inadequate. Gammage, the Chartist historian of Chartism, who was present, remarked that many Chartists were greatly disappointed by O'Connor's poor showing.[5]

In his heart Feargus himself seems to have known that he had been out-argued. For after the Northampton meeting with characteristic impetuosity he changed from warm abuse to warm praise of Cobden. 'He is decidedly a man of genius,' he suddenly admitted in the *Northern Star* of August 10, 1844, 'of reflection, of talent, and of tact—and while he is in part deficient in some of those qualities which are necessary to constitute a good mob orator, he lacks none of those properties which entitle him to pre-eminence in the front rank of orators.'

His personal encounter with Cobden seems suddenly to have reminded O'Connor of the strength of the middle-class and of its leaders. After the Northampton meeting Feargus once again began to realise (as he had done temporarily in 1842) that the operatives needed a middle-class alliance, that the people lacked the strength to achieve reform alone.

In 1846 the Anti-Corn Law League achieved its objective. The Corn Laws were repealed, thanks at the last to the conversion of Sir Robert Peel. Peel's role at this time taught O'Connor another important lesson about the facts of contemporary politics. Even the middle-classes had needed the assistance of an established parliamentary figure to carry repeal through parliament. O'Connor now realised that the working-classes would equally need such assistance if any of the reforms which they desired were to be achieved. At the end of 1845 O'Connor changed his line on

4. *Northern Star*, Feb. 3—March 23, 1844.
5. *Northern Star*, *The League*, Aug. 10, 1844; Gammage, *Chartist Movement*, 253-55.

Peel with the same abruptness as he had earlier changed his line on Cobden. To the surprise of many Chartists he began fulsomely to praise Peel. O'Connor tried to persuade himself and his followers that Peel's policy, which had been increasingly reformist during the course of his great ministry, might in the end satisfy many of the Chartist demands. Repeal of the Corn Laws was an 'all-mighty measure', 'an instalment of the concessions which, sooner or later must, and will be made, to the democratic mind of this country.' By reducing the price of land it would facilitate progress of the Land Plan. Peel's reform ministry had been 'the most daring, and statesmanlike, of which the annals of the country bear record': 'For five years Peel has led an incipient Chartist movement.'[6]

After his return to parliament in 1847 O'Connor showed Peel most uncharacteristic deference, as for example when he spoke in 1848 on the Irish Coercion Bill:[7]

> The right hon. Baronet differed from him in politics, and perhaps the right hon. Baronet would take that as a compliment. But he would say of the right hon. Baronet, that his firm conviction was, if he had been at the helm last year and this, there would have been no need to ask for Coercion Bills. They said it was dangerous to compliment the right hon. Baronet; but he must say that he was the only man to whom the moneyed classes and the people of the country looked as the man that could save the country.

When Peel died in 1850 the *Northern Star* shared in the general mourning. Peel's portrait was given away to readers just as in earlier years the paper had given away portraits of working-class Radical leaders. O'Connor had learnt that the skilful advocacy of an established parliamentarian such as Peel was as vital to the success of popular agitation as all the noise of demagogue agitators, himself among them.[8]

---

6. *Northern Star*, Dec. 20, 1845, Jan. 31, July 4, 1846; Gammage, *Chartist Movement*, 270.

7. *Parliamentary Debates*, third series, C (1848), 715.

8. *Northern Star*, July 6, 1850.

CHAPTER XIII

ENGLAND AND IRELAND, 1843-47

On September 27, 1841 O'Connor attended a Chartist meeting at Manchester to welcome him on his release from jail. At this meeting he made an important gesture in his persistent quest for Irish support. He told his audience that a local Irishman had called upon him that morning and asked him to give up advocating physical force and abusing Daniel O'Connell. Feargus had answered that he had never advocated physical force; he had not replied to the request about Daniel O'Connell, but he did so publicly now. 'Hear me, then, Englishmen, Irishmen, and Scotchmen, if it is to take away the pretext for dissension and to gratify Irishmen, I pledge myself not even to mention the name of Daniel O'Connell, so long as he abstains from abusing Chartists and the Charter.' Feargus asked the people simply to begin comparing O'Connell and himself and to judge for themselves whose policy was the better for 'allaying grievances, promoting union, and establishing freedom.'[1]

Writing in the *Northern Star* at the beginning of 1843 O'Connor reminded the Irish people how he had kept his promise during the past fifteen months, even though O'Connell had not in fact given up his attacks upon the Chartists. Now, however, he noted that O'Connell seemed to be moving towards Chartism, having started an intensive agitation for repeal of the Union, and also for fixity of land tenure, abolition of tithes, extended suffrage, shorter parliaments, abolition of the property qualification, and equal electoral districts. This programme, O'Connor pointed out, was largely the one which he had been urging O'Connell to agitate for ten years:[2]

---

1. *Northern Star*, Oct. 2, 1841.
2. Ibid, Jan. 14, 1843.

Alas! my friends, it is hard that I should have been branded a traitor to my country because I would not join in her sale or be a party to her degradation; but it is more than payment to find that my accuser and most implacable foe has been compelled to abandon his own, and acquiesce in my policy.

O'Connor offered the support of the Chartists for O'Connell's new repeal agitation. O'Connell, however, continued emphatically to reject all connection with O'Connor. When O'Connor and O'Brien joined a branch of the Repeal Association in London, O'Connell had them ejected and their entrance money returned.[3] Nevertheless, during 1843 O'Connor filled the *Northern Star* with his dream of a Chartist-Irish alliance. 'Spite of all attempts to separate the English from the Irish,' he wrote in an address to the Irish in England, published in the paper on June 10th, 'I will struggle to unite them.'

As it happened, O'Connell's day as the unassailable political leader of Ireland was now nearly over. A projected monster repeal meeting at Clontarf in October 1843 had to be ignominiously abandoned under a government prohibition, and thereafter O'Connell's predominance in Ireland began to break up. He withdrew the demand for total repeal and began to advocate federalism. This lost him the support of the more ardent Irish nationalists, the Young Ireland party. It also led O'Connor to resume his attacks upon O'Connell: 'we now tell that leader—and in telling him we speak the sentiments of the British masses, that *he shall have no assistance from them* FOR THE HUMBUG OF FEDERALISM.'[4]

O'Connell died in 1847. The Young Irelanders, Gavan Duffy, John Mitchel and others, took over leadership of the Irish movement. Would they work with O'Connor? They were at least as ardent for repeal as Feargus, but no more than O'Connell were they impressed by him. They regarded him not as a sincere Irish patriot but as an unprincipled demagogue. In addition, they disliked Chartist principles, for they were not democrats. In August 1846 *The Nation,* the newspaper of Young Ireland, made it clear that the new Irish party did not want Chartist support:

---

3. O'Higgins, Ireland and Chartism, 199-200.
4. *Northern Star,* Oct. 21, 1843.

We desire no fraternisation between the Irish people and the Chartists, not on account of the bugbear of physical force, but simply because some of their five points are to us an abomination, and the whole spirit and tone of their proceedings, though well enough for England, are so essentially English that their adoption in Ireland would neither be probable nor at all desirable. Between us and them there is a gulf fixed, and we desire, not to bridge it over, but to make it wider and deeper.

The *Northern Star* reprinted this passage and published a series of editorials in reply to prove the wisdom of the Chartist six points and their importance for Ireland as well as England.[5]

The removal of O'Connell thus did little to help O'Connor towards his dream of an Anglo-Irish working-class alliance with himself at its head. Despite all rebuffs, however, Feargus continued to take a close interest in Irish affairs. This became very apparent after he entered parliament in 1847.

The return of O'Connor as second member for Nottingham was the great surprise of the general election of July 1847. Nottingham had always been a strong Chartist centre, and as we have seen, O'Connor was a favourite there. But only a few hundred Chartists in the town had the vote. O'Connor seems to have owed his success not to Chartist but to Tory support, along with middle-class Radical abstentions. Walter, the Tory candidate polled 1,830 votes, O'Connor got 1,340. Many Tories seem to have given their second votes to O'Connor in order to keep out the Whig candidates, Gisborne who received 1,081 votes and Sir John Hobhouse, a cabinet minister, who got only 974. Many former supporters of Gisborne and Hobhouse seem to have abstained. Gisborne had been elected as a Radical and had disappointed his supporters by his mildness. Hobhouse was associated in the eyes of the numerous local nonconformists with the recent government education proposals, which the dissenters believed to favour the Anglicans. Hobhouse himself blamed his defeat upon his refusal to bribe, as he had done freely at previous elections.

O'Connor's programme seems to have been designed to avoid alarming those Radical electors who were thinking of abstaining.

---

5. *Northern Star*, Aug. 29—Oct. 17, 1846; C. G. Duffy, *Four Years of Irish History* (1883), 449-50.

It said little of Chartism; it demanded an education system which recognised sectarian differences (plainly a sop to the local nonconformists); it asked for complete free trade, for repeal of the Irish union and for a grant of land for 'each willing husbandman.'[6] After his victory O'Connor wrote to T. S. Duncombe, the Radical who had presented the National Petition in 1842, promising to accept his leadership in the Commons:[7]

> I will propose no national question of which you are the proper, the acknowledged, the loved leader; nor shall adversity or prosperity ever banish from my recollection the boldness of the friend who visited me in my *dungeon*. My service is not like that of any other man when I give it; life itself is offered, if needed.

Feargus made one important qualification to this characteristically exaggerated offer of support. He asked for freedom to act as he pleased on Irish questions. And in fact during his first months in parliament he spoke mainly on Irish questions. As in 1833 he spoke about Ireland on the address. He contended that the Irish famine had shattered the old Irish land system; he hoped that the opportunity would be taken to introduce fixity of tenure. He urged the Irish members, much divided since the decline and death of O'Connell, to sink their differences. He clearly hoped to lead them himself. 'He should consider himself as a soldier in the cause of Ireland, although not now resident there, and he would sit in that House, stand in that House, and sleep in that House until they succeeded.' He resisted a Whig Coercion Bill, and in December he moved for a select committee to inquire into the effects of the Union upon Ireland.[8]

As well as trying to establish his leadership over the Irish members of parliament, Feargus also tried to re-establish his

6. *Nottingham Review, Nottingham Journal,* July 23, 30; Northern Star, July 24, 31, 1847; A. C. Wood, 'Nottingham 1835-1865', *Trans. Thoroton Society,* LIX (1955), 76-81.

7. T. H. Duncombe, *Life and Correspondence of Thomas Slingsby Duncombe* (1868), I, 373.

8. *Parliamentary Debates,* third series, XCV (1847), 141-43, 752-65, 796-97; R. D. Edwards & T. O. Williams (eds.), *The Great Famine* (1956), 183-84.

influence in Co. Cork. He unsuccessfully attempted about this time to buy the *Cork Southern Reporter*. Had he succeeded he would no doubt have made it an Irish counterpart of the *Northern Star*.[9]

Thus Ireland and her problems were as much in the mind of O'Connor as the problems of England as he entered 1848, the 'Year of Revolutions.:[10]

> *'Ireland for the Irish!'* and *'England for the English!'* is the mutual cry. Let it be shouted, side by side—from John o'Groats to Connemara—from the Giant's Causeway to the Cliffs of Dover—it will be the knell of oppression—it will be the birth-peal of freedom—for the solitary fortresses of tyranny must sink before the confluence of our united nations.

9. *Fraser's Magazine*, XXXVII (1848), 174.
10. *Northern Star*, Dec. 11, 1847.

CHAPTER XIV

1848 AND AFTER

As 1848 opened, economic distress, the basic ingredient of political discontent, was widespread throughout England and Ireland. The prosperity of 1843-45 had been followed by the Irish famine and by the financial crisis of 1847. 'Christmas! The very word brings visions of plenteous boards,' commented the *Northern Star* on Christmas Day 1847, '—of full bowls and blazing logs, faces of merriment and hearts of joy. Plenteous boards there will be— but not for the poor.' For the poor there was only the knowledge that 1848 was 'a year of promise,' a year when the Charter might be achieved.

Within a few weeks this promise was fleetingly to seem very great to the *Northern Star* and to Feargus O'Connor, as Europe was shaken by revolutions and as a new monster Chartist petition was prepared for presentation to parliament. The excited mood on the continent added to the Chartist excitement in England. Relations between revolutionaries in Europe and Chartist leaders in England had become quite close in the years immediately before 1848. Harney, now editor of the *Northern Star,* gave much space to continental movements. O'Connor himself was less interested in foreign revolutionaries, but he did have some contacts with them. He visited Western Europe in 1845 to compare systems of smallholding in preparation for launching his Land Plan. He then met Marx, and in July 1846 Marx and Engels sent him a congratulatory address on his campaign at a bye-election in Nottingham. He had defeated Hobhouse, the Whig candidate, on the show of hands (although he did not on this occasion go to the poll, as in the following year):[1]

---

1. *Northern Star,* Sept. 20--Oct. 11, 1845, July 25, 1846.

We consider this, Sir, as a sign that the working classes of England are very well aware of the position they have to take after the triumph of Free-Trade. We conclude from this fact that they know very well that now, when the middle-classes have carried their chief measure, when they have only to replace the present weak go-between cabinet by an energetical, really middle-class ministry, in order to be acknowledged the ruling class of your country, that now the great struggle of capital and labour, of *bourgeois* and *proletarian,* must come to a decision.

Marx and Engels promised to extend the circulation of the *Northern Star* on the continent and to have extracts translated in as many continental newspapers as possible.

But O'Connor did not really share Marx's view of the inevitable class struggle. As we have shown, the lesson of free trade for him was that the working-classes must work not against the powerful middle-classes but with them if they wished to obtain reform.

Yet in the excitement of 1848 O'Connor again temporarily forgot this lesson, as he had already once forgotten it after the excitement of the Plug Strikes in 1842. Once again he was tempted to lead a separate movement of the operatives. He found the temptation irresistible because at the beginning of 1848 it seemed as if his long-held hope of an Anglo-Irish working-class alliance might at last be fulfilled. A section of the Young Ireland party changed its attitude to Chartism. At the end of 1847 John Mitchel resigned from *The Nation,* launched an agitation of his own and began openly to urge the Irish people to revolution. He was still no democrat, but he decided that an alliance between the Irish in Ireland and England and the Chartists might be useful. In January 1848 and again in April conferences were held of Irish Confederates and Irish Chartists, at which Chartist delegates from England were present. In Dublin the Irish Universal Suffrage Association revived. In England, notably in London and Manchester, Irish residents who had previously been hostile to the local Chartists now began to associate with them.[2]

O'Connor was delighted by this new trend. He praised Mitchel in the *Northern Star.* 'Many laughed at the extravagant notion of a union ever being formed between the English and the Irish

2. O'Higgins, Ireland and Chartism, 147-55, 203-31, 274-78.

working classes . . . Who will now doubt that a union of brave and sympathising hearts is about to take place?' On St. Patrick's Day, March 17th, accompanied by Meagher and Doheny, Confederate delegates from Ireland, O'Connor spoke at a meeting in the Free Trade Hall, Manchester, at which the local Irish Confederates and the local Chartists proclaimed their alliance:

> If I were to ask you what brought you here to-night, and if I were to receive a true and consistent answer, that answer should be—to receive absolution from me. (Cheers.) For now thirteen years I have been advocating the very union which you have thus tardily confirmed—and when I proposed that union against adverse circumstances, . . . I was told the day would never arrive when Englishmen and Irishmen would stand together upon the same platform, advocating the same principles. (Cheers.) I thank God I have lived to see the day.

The next evening an Anglo-Irish soirée was held in Manchester Town Hall. 'If last night was the wedding,' remarked O'Connor, 'they might look upon that as the honeymoon.' On the following day, a Sunday, an Anglo-Irish camp meeting was held on Oldham Edge. 'Help us . . . to get Ireland for the Irish,' asked Doheny, 'and we will help you to get England for the English.' 'What he had often prophesied had come to pass,' exclaimed O'Connor joyfully, 'that the people of both countries must unite before the oppressors of both would give liberty to both.'[3]

Excited by the occasion Feargus drifted into ambiguous language, just as he had done during the excitement of 1838-39 and 1842:

> If there should come dark and black and sanguinary news from Ireland, he told the Oldham gathering, 'he should not confine his defence of Ireland to the House of Commons. He did not know how the people of England would feel if he were to-morrow or the next day seized by the law, attempting to do justice to them. He did not know how his children (the people) would feel if their father was torn from them.

As in 1838-39 and 1842 the more ardent Chartists began to arm themselves and to drill upon the moors.

---

3. *Northern Star*, March 18, 25, 1848.

9

Yet in his elation at the new Irish connection O'Connor glossed over its limited nature. A section only of the Irish leaders had decided to work with the Chartists, and only for reasons of expediency. Mitchel and his friends had not adopted Chartist principles. Still less were they prepared to acknowledge O'Connor's leadership. They continued to distrust and to dislike him personally. Doheny wrote to his wife after the Oldham Edge meeting that 'the only drawback was Feargus O'Connor ... He spattered so much about *his* character and *his* teaching and *his* everything.'[4] Even if all had gone well, O'Connor would not have found himself accepted as the great leader of the English and Irish people. After things went wrong at the Kennington Common meeting of April 10th the Confederates quickly threw him over and went their own way.

The Kennington Common demonstration was intended to be the climax of the renewed Chartist campaign. For a third time a National Petition had been organised and a National Convention elected to support it. The idea of the Chartists was to march from the meeting in force to deliver the petition at the House of Commons where O'Connor himself would present it. Recent revolutions on the continent had set the nerves of propertied people on edge. They feared that the meeting was intended to mark the beginning of the English revolution. O'Connor's language in the weeks before the meeting was certainly not likely to calm them. He told the National Convention ambiguously on April 5th that 'he was not prepared to destroy the movement he had been mainly instrumental in raising by precipitation, nor was he prepared to allow the people to remain in bondage one moment longer than they could obtain their freedom.' He claimed that the disturbed state of Ireland would keep all the army busy there. He concluded that as 'he was now becoming a quasi-minister,' he would doubtless be asked what the Chartists intended to do on Monday, April 10th. 'On the faith of that Convention, he should reply, that not one pane of glass, nor one penny-worth of property would be injured. (Loud cheers)'. In the event of the rejection of the National Petition he recommended calling simultaneous meetings.

---

4. P.R.O. (Dublin), Chief Secretary's Office Unregistered Papers (1848), carton 1523 (105/26), quoted O'Higgins, Ireland and Chartism, 217.

These should send up petitions to the Queen asking her to discuss the present government and to appoint one favourable to the Charter:[5]

> If that were unavailing, he would never flinch, but would sooner die than not win the Charter. He meant to wait no longer than the time when the majority of the people demanded it—and were prepared to establish their rights. He thought they now had the power to obtain it.

On April 1st O'Connor addressed the Chartist 'Old Guards' in the *Northern Star*. He swore loyalty to the Charter and to the Land Plan. 'I would not give a fig for the Charter if we were not prepared with a solid, social system to take the place of the artificial one which we mean to destroy.' Alongside this address on the front page of the paper was a plan drawn up by Feargus for a peasant democratic republic. He suggested it for France. He assured the 'Old Guards' that his exiled uncle Arthur was about to become president of the new French Republic. He denied that he had similar ambitions for himself in England.

By this time O'Connor was in a state of excessive excitement. He did not really know how much or how little he was threatening. He had worked himself into a similar state in the winter of 1838-39. He became seriously ill then, and the same happened now. And as in 1839 the authorities pricked the bubble. On April 6th a proclamation was issued forbidding the proposed procession to the House of Commons as calculated to intimidate the House. The Duke of Wellington was called in to advise the cabinet on defence measures, and troops poured into London. These were, however, kept out of sight; the aim of the authorities was if possible to control the situation by using only police and special constables. According to *The Times*, a hundred and fifty thousand of the latter were enrolled, showing the readiness of the propertied classes to defend themselves.

In the face of this firm resistance, and worn out by over-excitement, O'Connor suddenly lost his nerve. For six nights before the meeting he hardly slept; his chest complaint of 1839 recurred. He now became abjectly conciliatory. He assured the House of Commons that he would not allow the meeting to assemble if he

---

5. *Northern Star*, April 8, 1848.

thought a single breach of the peace likely to occur. He would be unworthy of a seat in the House if he had any intention of attempting to overawe it by a demonstration.[6] Forgetting all his own recent strong language, he denounced those whose threats and arming had given the authorities the impression that intimidation of parliament was intended. In the National Convention on the morning of the meeting he actually began to excuse the government for banning the procession :[7]

> Now, he would wish the Convention to put themselves into the place of the Government, and say whether if they had heard that an armed demonstration was to take place, they would not have felt it their duty to meet it, and endeavour to prevent the peace being destroyed?—Had it not been for the folly of some persons out of the Convention—and a few in it—there would never have been any opposition to their demonstration.

On the night before the meeting Thomas Allsop, a Radical stockbroker, who had helped to finance the Land Plan, and who had provided O'Connor with the necessary property qualification for parliament, wrote to Feargus describing what he thought would be the best line of conduct during and after the meeting :[8]

> Nothing rashly. The government must be met with calm and firm defiance. Violence may be overcome with violence, but a resolute determination not to submit cannot be overcome. To remain in front, *en face* of the government, to watch it, to take advantage of its blunders, is the part of an old general who will not be guided like a fish by its tail. Precipitate nothing, yield nothing. Aim not alone to destroy the government, but to render a class government impossible. No hesitation, no rash impulse, no egotism; but an earnest, serious, unyielding progress. Nothing for self, nothing even for fame, present or posthumous. All for the cause . . . Upon the elevation of your course for the moment will depend the estimation in which you will henceforth be held; and the position you may attain and retain will be second to none of the reformers who have gone before you.

---

6. *Parliamentary Debates*, third series, XCVII (1848), 1354-55; XCVIII (1848), 11-13.

7. *Northern Star*, April 15, 1848.

8. *D.N.B., sub* Allsop, Thomas.

This was wise advice. A policy of non-violence in this mood might have had an effect. But the mood would have been difficult to create, and on April 10th O'Connor was incapable of attempting to create it.

Yet on the morning of April 10th the Chartist rank and file were not yet aware of O'Connor's chastened attitude. Most of them probably had no clear idea what they expected to happen; they simply put their trust in O'Connor. During the late morning processions marched to Kennington Common from all parts of London; among them was a procession of Irish Confederates with a banner demanding 'Ireland for the Irish.' The shops were shut; the 'respectable' classes waited for trouble. Estimates of the numbers at the meeting varied widely. O'Connor afterwards claimed four to five hundred thousand; *The Times* said twenty thousand, of whom only half were active participants. Lord John Russell, the Prime Minister, told the Queen that twelve to fifteen thousand people were present. These lower estimates were probably nearer the truth than O'Connor's. The numbers seem to have been much less than the Chartists had hoped.

The procession of National Convention delegates left their meeting place in John Street just before 10 a.m. This procession was headed by a car carrying the National Petition drawn by four horses and decorated with red, green and white tricolour flags. O'Connor sat on the first seat of a second car, accompanied by Ernest Jones, Harney and other leading protégés. When this procession reached Kennington Common the people were already assembled. O'Connor's car began to cross the common, but on its way a messenger came up from Mayne, the Commissioner of Police, asking O'Connor to have a word with him before the meeting. Feargus readily agreed and left the common. Few of the people knew why he was going, and a cry went round 'They have got him.' There was a rush forward. This was the nearest the meeting was to come to violence. Then gradually the rush subsided, and the people waited. O'Connor met Mayne in a nearby tavern. According to Russell's account to the Queen, Feargus looked pale and frightened. Mayne told him that the meeting could continue, but that no procession would be allowed to cross the Thames bridges to take the petition to the House of Commons. O'Connor thanked him effusively, begging to shake him by the hand. The people were of course unaware of this curious interlude, and when Feargus returned to the meeting they met him with a tremendous shout. He mounted his car and began his speech. He had come to the meeting, he announced, despite threats on his life. For a quarter of a century he had agitated for democracy; he was therefore entitled to be followed by the people when he begged them now to maintain peace. 'Let me enjoin—nay, I would go down on my knees to beseech you—do not now destroy the cause I have struggled for all my life.' The procession would have to be given up. He asked those who were willing to accept this advice to hold up their hands. A mass of hands was immediately raised. O'Connor thus carried the meeting with him. But he had virtually presented the policy of peace as a policy of retreat before the government. This was not the mood recommended by Allsop of peace accompanied by 'resolute determination not to submit.' O'Connor was unfit to do better.

After his speech O'Connor left the meeting in a cab—hardly a triumphant departure—and went to the Home Office where he repeated to Sir George Grey, the Home Secretary, his assurance that the crowd would disperse quietly. Grey told him that he had done rightly but that the force at the bridges to prevent access to the Westminster side would be maintained. According to Russell's account to the Queen, O'Connor then replied, 'Not a man should be taken away. The Government have been quite right. I told the Convention that if they had been the Government they never would have allowed such a meeting.'

Soon after O'Connor's departure the meeting had broken up into fragments which were separately addressed by several Chartist leaders. By a quarter to two the crowds had dispersed. Three cabs drew up on the common, the bales of the National Petition were put inside them, and O'Connor drove with them to the House of Commons. Thus ignominiously the National Petition reached parliament.[9]

O'Connor claimed that the petition had 5,706,000 signatures. But on April 13th a committee of scrutineers reported that it had in fact only 1,975,496 signatures, including many fictitious ones such as 'Victoria Rex,' 'Duke of Wellington,' 'No Cheese,' &c.

9. *The Times,* April 11; *Northern Star,* April 15, 1848; Frost, *Forty Years' Recollections,* 136-41; Lord John Russell to Queen Victoria, April 10, 1848 (2 p.m.), (*Letters of Queen Victoria* (1908), II, 168-69).

That such a monster petition had many spurious signatures was not really surprising. O'Connor might have passed this off. He might even have accepted the reduction in the number of genuine signatures to less than two million, emphasising that the petition still represented an impressive weight of public opinion. Instead, he excitedly threw away his case, challenging a particularly carping member of the committee to a dual. He was arrested by the Serjeant-at-Arms and forced, with his opponent, to apologise to the House. This affair added to the ridicule now surrounding the petition and the whole Chartist movement in 'respectable' circles.[10]

O'Connor tried hard to prove to himself and to the Chartists that the Kennington meeting was a great victory. He assured the National Convention on April 12th that he had received hundreds of congratulatory letters from all parts of the country for his conduct at the meeting. But later in the same speech he lapsed into admitting that the meeting had failed. 'The ministers supposed they had achieved a triumph over the people on Monday, but if they had it would only prove evanescent ... It was the folly of their own people (the Chartists) that had led to the chance of a collision on Monday, for if strong language had not been used on the part of those connected with them, there would have been no resistance to the procession.'[11]

But the most significant admission of failure made by O'Connor was his sudden change of policy after the meeting. The people had again tried to agitate alone and had again failed. A major reason for their defeat had been the solidarity of the middle-classes. *The Times* claimed that the number of special constables enrolled in London outnumbered the Chartists present at the meeting by fifteen to one. The propertied classes had again proved their power. And O'Connor now turned once more to them. In the *Northern Star* of April 22nd he again began to advocate a Chartist alliance with the middle-classes. He claimed that the demonstration of April 10th and the pressure of trade depression had converted many of the middle-classes to Radicalism. 'One half of my time since has been devoted to reading the most kindly and affectionate letters from shopkeepers, tradesmen, and others of the middle classes, tendering their hearty co-operation to the

10. *Parliamentary Debates*, third series, XCVIII (1848), 284-301.
11. *Northern Star*, April 15, 1848.

popular cause.' O'Connor stressed that 'fraternisation' with the middle-classes would not mean abandonment of the Charter. The Chartists must keep their movement and their demands intact. But he now urged the people to work with the middle-classes for reform as far as the middle-classes would go. In this spirit he began to support during the summer of 1848 the new 'Little Charter' movement of Bright and Hume which sought household suffrage and triennial parliaments.

O'Connor's advocacy of a middle-class alliance was still liable to periods of relapse—when he returned to abuse of the middle-class leaders. The lesson that he had slowly learnt, that he would have to follow Bright and Cobden, was not an easy one to accept; but for the remaining few years of his political career Feargus adhered to this policy more or less. At the beginning of 1849 the middle-class reformers founded a Parliamentary and Financial Reform Association, which sought both parliamentary reform and economy in government expenditure. O'Connor told a meeting of the association at Norwich on October 3, 1849 that:

> He was happy to say that throughout England and Scotland, every Chartist had now fraternised with the middle classes in this movement . . . True, he had on previous occasions opposed the middle-class movements—he had opposed them in free trade, and had advised the Chartists not to join in that agitation—but that was not because he was not a free trader, but because he knew that free trade in legislation was the first thing necessary before they could carry out any other free trade measure for the benefit of the people.

He did not support the new association because of its interest in financial reform—the people would not benefit from reduced expenditure alone—but because the association had taken up four of the principles of the Charter: 'and if they once obtained those they would have a quadruped to go upon in their efforts to obtain the remaining points.' Ireland was still in his mind. He was glad that a previous middle-class speaker had not confined his strictures to English misrepresentation but had included Ireland:[12]

> There was a country with an industrious people, an honest and sagacious people with idle land, idle labour, and idle

---

12. *Northern Star,* Oct. 6, 1849; Gammage, *Chartist Movement,* 347-50.

money, industry checked, nay prohibited by the sway of feudal lords, and the nation represented by lickspittals in the House of Commons.

O'Connor had learnt the lesson of his own failure and was now anxious to teach it to the people; but having realised the magnitude of his past mistakes, the people were not now prepared to accept O'Connor as their leader in new directions. After the Kennington Common fiasco, followed by the Land Plan revelations, support for Chartism and for O'Connor fell rapidly away. By October 28, 1848 the *Northern Star* was forced to admit that 'popular indifference was never more clearly manifested than at the present time.'

Even within the reduced Chartist movement O'Connor was no longer dominant. In the *Northern Star* of April 22nd he had denounced as illegal a proposal to call a Chartist National Assembly. Despite his opposition the assembly met on May 1st, and during its debates O'Connor's leadership was frequently attacked. Harney and Ernest Jones were warned by O'Connor that if they attended they would lose their jobs on the *Northern Star*. Harney reluctantly acquiesced, but Jones left. O'Connor's lieutenants were beginning to break away. Votes of confidence in O'Connor were passed at meetings in many places, and eventually a reconciliation was patched up between him and the assembly. But O'Connor's leadership was no longer secure.[13]

The physical force Chartists and the Irish Confederates now proceeded to act without O'Connor. The failure of April 10th did not seriously dismay the Confederates, who, as we have seen, were not deeply committed to O'Connor's movement. They now planned a rising in association with the Chartist extremists. The plot centred in the North of England. This had been O'Connor's stronghold, but now even in Barnsley, where his influence over English and Irish had been particularly great, his new policy of middle-class alliance was ignored and preparations made for a rising. The *Sheffield Independent* reported on April 29th that pike blades were being carried through the streets of Barnsley to be ground 'as openly as cutlers in Sheffield carry their work through the streets ... It is quite amusing to hear the children

---

13. *Northern Star,* May 6, 13, 1848; Gammage, *Chartist Movement,* 224-26; Schoyen, *Chartist Challenge,* 167-69.

quarrel among themselves as to the quality of their father' pikes, and to see them sketch the shape of them on the causeway.'

On at least two occasions a date was fixed for simultaneous risings of the English and Irish people, first for June 12th and then for August 15th. But the government had the situation in hand, and mass arrests prevented both outbreaks.

These desperate last attempts had no general support. The majority of working men had turned away from Chartism. Many more withdrew from the movement in 1849 when trade again revived. Speaking at Nottingham in September 1850 O'Connor complained that when trade was bad the operatives cried out to be led; but when trade improved and they had 8s. or 10s. a week in their pockets they became indifferent to politics, at the very time when they were best able to maintain agitation.[14]

At this period O'Connor was making a last effort to revive the Chartist movement and to bring English and Irish working-classes together. Earlier in the year he had been prominent in the establishment in Dublin of an Irish Democratic Association. The *Northern Star* looked forward optimistically to 'the foundation of a cordial and lasting union between Radical Reformers on both sides of the Channel.' But the new body was opposed by Duffy and the Irish Alliance, and as a result its influence in Ireland was slight.[15]

O'Connor was never to realise his dream of a great alliance of English operatives and Irish peasants. After his repudiation by Daniel O'Connell he was never able to re-establish his influence over the Irish peasants. Now his influence over the English working men was also largely gone. At the end of 1850 at a new election for the Chartist executive, O'Connor, instead of heading the poll as in the past, came out only fifth. And even this, remarked Gammage, the Chartist historian of Chartism, was probably on compassionate grounds. For under the excitement and disappointment of these last years O'Connor had gone gradually out of his mind.[16]

---

14. *Nottingham Review*, Sept. 6, 1850.
15. *Northern Star*, March 16, 1850; O'Higgins, Ireland and Chartism, 156-61.
16. *Northern Star*, Dec. 21, 1850; Gammage, *Chartist Movement*, 358.

CHAPTER XV

PRIVATE LIFE

O'Connor's career had been one of continuous and excessive activity and excitement, difficulty and disappointment. His father had probably been mad for the latter part of his life, and by the end of the 1840s Feargus's own mind was beginning to give way. Throughout his Chartist career O'Connor was frequently ill. Early in 1839, as we have seen, he seems to have nearly died from inflammation of the chest. Just before his imprisonment in 1840 he was delirious for four nights. He thought he was being followed by a hedgehog :

> At length I ran it down; and, in endeavouring to catch it, its bristles stuck to the palm of my hand, from which I could not disengage them, and in that situation I made my way to the Queen's Bench, where I saw the Attorney-General without his wig, and who, the moment I entered, claimed the hedgehog as his wig, charged me with the theft, and put me upon my trial for the offence.[1]

O'Connor was ill in prison of 'a severe nervous fever' and also with rheumatism. In October 1840 a rumour of his death spread through the Manchester area. Because of ill-health he was released from jail early. At the beginning of 1845 he was incapacitated for five weeks with inflammation of one of his eyes, and in November of that year he was again seriously unwell. He told the Kennington Common meeting of 1848 that he had a blister on his chest : 'my breast at this moment, is like a coal of fire.' In the spring of 1850 he was ill for some weeks.[2]

---

1. *Northern Star*, May 23, 1840.
2. Ibid, Aug. 1, Oct, 31, 1840, Jan. 11, 18, Nov. 29, 1845, April 15, 1848; *The Times*, April 11, 1848; *Parliamentary Debates*, third series, CX (1850), 496.

O'Connor's constitution thus seems to have been seriously undermined by his exceptional activity in the Chartist cause. To keep himself going he turned increasingly to drink. By the time of his final breakdown in 1852 he was drinking fifteen glasses of brandy a day. By the end of the '40s his red hair had turned white and his face was haggard.[3]

O'Connor had always been an exhibitionist, and for long his incipient insanity was taken to be only more marked exhibitionism. His liking in his last years for conspicuous dress was long regarded in this light. He was remembered about 1850 wearing 'the old-fashioned nankeen breeches, or trousers, buckled shoes, a blue coat with brass or gilt buttons, a light vest, and a white or cream-coloured hat.'[4]

In the *Northern Star* of December 13, 1851 an anonymous contributor suggested that O'Connor should withdraw from public life 'until his constitution has recovered from the shock which the enemies to his Land Scheme have chiefly occasioned.' By this date it was at last becoming widely realised that he was mentally unbalanced. At a banquet given in October 1851 to Kossuth, the Hungarian patriot, Feargus went up to him, seized him by the hand and greeted him with exaggerated effusiveness.[5] He attended the Court of Chancery, where the affairs of the Land Company were being wound up, and made humorous interruptions. In the House of Commons he mimicked the Speaker and slapped Lord Palmerston on the back just as he was about to address the House. Justin McCarthy saw him wandering about Covent Garden market in these last days, 'his eyes gleaming with the peculiar, quick, shallow, ever-changing glitter of madness. The poor fellow rambled from fruit-stall to fruit-stall, talking all the while to himself, sometimes taking up a fruit as if he meant to buy it, and then putting it down with a vacant laugh and walking on.'[6]

---

3. *Gentleman's Magazine*, new series, XLIV (1855), 547; Frost, *Forty Years' Recollections*, 183-84; *Fraser's Magazine*, XXXVII (1848), 175.
4. W. Tinsley, *Random Recollections of an Old Publisher* (1900), I, 44.
5. Gammage, *Chartist Movement*, 377-78.
6. J. McCarthy, *Reminiscences* (1899), II, 259-61.

In the spring of 1852 O'Connor's friends began to take steps to have him put in an asylum. To avoid this Feargus sailed hurriedly for the United States. He went into a New York store, chucked a pretty woman under the chin and asked her how she would like a moustache. He was ejected.[7]

O'Connor returned to England early in June 1852. On June 8th during a debate in the Commons he struck a fellow member and had to apologise to the House. On the next day he struck another member. The House decided that he must be put under restraint, and the Serjeant-at-Arms was ordered to arrest O'Connor, who had left the chamber. The Serjeant obviously did not relish the task, for in February Feargus had been imprisoned for seven days for assaulting a policeman. But in the event O'Connor allowed himself to be quietly arrested in Westminster Hall and confined in an apartment in the Palace of Westminster. His sister, Harriet, petitioned for his release so that he could be put in an asylum. A select committee of the Commons was appointed. Dr. Harrington Tuke, a pioneer in the treatment of the insane, was called before it and certified that O'Connor was out of his mind. On June 16, 1852 the Commons agreed that O'Connor should be transferred to Tuke's asylum at Chiswick. Feargus went readily, under the impression that he was a state prisoner merely lodging with Tuke. Under this impression he always remained.[8]

O'Connor might have retained his sanity even under the stress disappointment of his public career if he had enjoyed a settled private life. During the 1820s he had been happy running his Fort Robert estate, but after he entered parliament in 1832 he never enjoyed a settled home life again. He never married, even though in his younger days he must have seemed an eligible bachelor. He did come near to marriage on the eve of his election to parliament in 1832, but the glorious political career which he outlined to the lady did not banish her suspicion that his motive was money rather than love. Soon afterwards he tried to borrow

---

7. *The Times,* May 26, 1852.
8. *Parliamentary Debates,* third series, CXIX (1852), 252, CXXII (1852), 273-74, 367-73; *Gentleman's Magazine,* new series, XLIV (1855), 546-47; McCarthy, *Reminiscences,* II, 260-61.

money from her to set up a beer and porter brewery at Fort Robert, a scheme designed to overcome his financial embarrassments. This further proposal, which she also rejected, no doubt confirmed her suspicions.[9]

As the Chartist leader, O'Connor seems to have had a marked influence over the wives of the operatives. Working women found his character attractive. In a letter 'to the Women of England' in 1847 Feargus assured the wives and mothers of the Chartists how much he appreciated their assistance in inducing their menfolk to subscribe to the Land Plan.[10]

O'Connor's relations with the opposite sex during these years were not only political. The warm blood of his family seems to have led him into a succession of affairs. In the early Chartist period it was noted that his speaking tours tended to follow the route of a celebrated actress, Louisa Nisbett, a woman of great beauty. Early in 1839 the rumour went round that the pair had married. No marriage in fact took place, but in his very last days Mrs. Nisbett was said to have been among those who nursed O'Connor, which suggested a real attachment between them.[11]

O'Connor had several illegitimate children. Edward O'Connor Terry, born in London on March 10, 1844, to a painter's wife seems to have inherited some histrionic talent from his father; for he achieved celebrity as a musical comedy actor, opening Terry's Theatre in London in 1887. He died in 1912.[12]

Throughout the Chartist period O'Connor was in financial difficulties, notwithstanding the large profits made at first by the *Northern Star*. He was forced to raise money upon his estate of Fort Robert, even though it was already heavily mortgaged when he came into it. By the beginning of 1852, mainly because of extravagance but also partly because of what he had spent in the Chartist cause, O'Connor was almost penniless. A subscription

---

9. Daunt, 'Feargus O'Connor', *Young Ireland,* V (1879), 471.
10. *Northern Star,* Dec. 4, 1847.
11. *D.N.B., sub* Nisbett, Louisa. C.; W. E. Adams, *Memoirs of a Social Atom* (1903),208-9.
12. *Chambers's Biographical Dictionary,* (1956 ed.) sub Terry, E. O'C; Armytage, 'Chartist Land Colonies', *Agricultural History,* vol. 32 (1958), 96.

was started for him; but his popularity had gone and only £32 was collected, mostly from Nottingham.[13]

His Chartist activity made O'Connor into an absentee landlord of Fort Robert, a role which he had previously condemned, and his long absences led to deterioration of the estate. In 1841 he seems to have let out the property on lease. At the time of Queen Victoria's visit to Ireland in 1849 he facetiously apologised for being unable to invite her to Fort Robert as the furniture had been sold to meet the poor rates. This suggested that at this time Fort Robert was still O'Connor's property although unoccupied. Within a few years the house was in ruins. The shell stands to this day.[14]

By the time of his confinement in Tuke's asylum O'Connor had lost his Irish home and was almost penniless. Happily his mind was no longer aware of such misfortunes. Tuke reported that he made himself quite at home, 'and, as is invariably the case in this peculiar form of brain disease, expressed himself perfectly well and happy.'[15] Feargus lived over his past triumphs again. When Ernest Jones visited him in March 1853 he found O'Connor playing with Tuke's little boys. On seeing Jones, Feargus broke out into the 'Lion of Freedom,' the Chartist song written in 1841 to welcome him from prison and sung at his meetings thereafter. Jones found that O'Connor could not maintain a thread of conversation. In April 1853 O'Connor again recited the 'Lion of Freedom' to a Lunacy Commission sent to interview him.[16]

All treatment proved ineffective, and during 1853 O'Connor's constitution began to deteriorate rapidly. In June 1854 he had the first of several epileptic fits. In June 1855 he became completely helpless. In August his sister, Harriet, removed O'Connor from the asylum to her home in Notting Hill. His physical agonies in his last days were severe, but his mind was completely gone. On August 30, 1855 Feargus O'Connor died.[17]

---

13. Mortgages in Registry of Deeds, Dublin; F. O'Connor, *Reply to Mr. John Watkins's Charges* [1843], 17-18; Gammage, *Chartist Movement*, 390; Wilson, *Struggles of an Old Chartist*, 17.
14. *Northern Star*, July 28, 1849.
15. *Gentleman's Magazine*, new series, XLIV (1855), 547.
16. Wilson, *Struggles of an Old Chartist*, 24; *The Times*, April 13, 1853.
17. *Gentleman's Magazine*, new series, XLIV (1855), 545, 547; Daunt, *Life Spent for Ireland*, 127.

Curiously, no trace has been found either of a will or of letters of administration; but according to his cousin, O'Neill Daunt, Feargus left a will bequeathing everything to his nephew, Arthur.[18] Almost certainly everything meant nothing, for no money was available to pay even for O'Connor's funeral. However, although he had been largely forgotten while in Tuke's asylum, O'Connor's death revived his memory among working-class reformers. His funeral at Kensal Green Cemetery on September 10, 1855 was paid for by public subscription. William Lovett, forgetting past animosities, took a leading part in the arrangements. Despite rain the coffin was followed by a long procession of working people, some carrying banners inscribed 'He lived and died for us.' *The Times* estimated that fifteen to twenty thousand people crowded into the cemetery and that an equal number had to be kept outside by the police. William Jones delivered an appreciative but not exaggerated funeral oration. He truthfully remarked that O'Connor had sacrificed money and prospects and finally his sanity in the service of the people. 'Tyrants call him a demagogue —slaves, a madman—the rich call him a fool—and the indifferent multitude leave him to his fate; but liberty and humanity mingle their tears on his grave.'[19]

Two memorials to O'Connor were erected by popular subscription. Over his grave a tapering Gothic spire in carved granite was set up, probably in 1857. This can still be seen, as can a statue of O'Connor unveiled in the Arboretum at Nottingham on August 22, 1859.[20] Money for this statue, which cost £100, had been laboriously collected in small sums by the Nottingham Chartists. The likeness is an indifferent one, and the pedestal is disproportionately large for the figure. The sculptor was J. B. Robinson of Darley Dale. It bears the simple inscription;

Feargus O'Connor, Esq. M.P.
This statue was erected by his admirers.
1859.

---

18. Daunt, *Life Spent for Ireland*, 164.
19. *The Times*, Sept. 11, 1855; W. Jones, *Funeral Oration on Feargus O'Connor* (1855).
20. *Nottingham Review*, Aug. 26, *Nottingham Telegraph*, Aug. 27, 1859.

CHAPTER XVI

CONCLUSION

FEARGUS O'Connor has been severely judged by most historians.
Sir Llewellyn Woodward's *Oxford History,* the most popular sixth-
form text-book for the period, describes him as 'the ruin of the
chartist movement.'[1] Graham Wallas in his article in the
Dictionary of National Biography came to a similar conclusion.
Woodward, Wallas and the rest have all been influenced by the
writings of contemporaries hostile to O'Connor. Among working-
class politicians Francis Place, William Lovett and Thomas Cooper
all left fluent denunciations of him. Contemporary middle-class
politicians and writers, almost without exception, damned him.
Francis Place described O'Connor as[2]

> the most restless of them all, who, by his volubility, his
> recklessness of truth, his newspaper, his unparalleled impudence,
> and by means of the talkative mischievous [men], whom he
> either paid or combined with to enable to pay themselves,
> triumphed over every other agitator. His vanity could only be
> gratified, and his purse filled, by the course he had taken, and
> as he was the best qualified, best constituted man amongst
> the leaders for his purpose, so he, in a short time, pushed aside
> all his competitors, and reigned lord paramount ... He seems
> never to have had any of the feeling denominated principle,
> and is utterly ignorant of every principle of political economy.
> He seems to be, and always to have been, governed by a most
> rancorous disposition towards every person, and body of
> persons, whose conduct does not at every moment confirm to
> his notions; in other words, who does not at all times acknow-
> ledge him as his or their leader, and thus minister to his absurd
> vanity.

---

1. E. L. Woodward, *Age of Reform* (1949), 130.
2. Add. Mss., 27, 820 f.3, quoted H. Jephson, *The Platform* (1892),
   II, 255-56.

Harriet Martineau's character-sketch of O'Connor showed Victorian middle-class Radical smugness at its worst:[3]

> Feargus O'Connor, whose only escape from a charge of cruel fraud on his followers for a course of years, is in an admission of such senselessness and ignorance as have made him the worst enemy of those whom he professed to serve. It is very probable that from the moment when Feargus O'Connor first placed himself at the head of a Chartist procession to the last stoppage of his land scheme, he may have fancied himself a sort of saviour of the working-classes: but if so, he must bear the contempt and compassionate disapproval of all men of ordinary sense and knowledge, as the only alternative from their utter reprobation.

O'Connor's egocentricity can be conceded at once. He wanted to be the unquestioned leader. Yet can mass movements be effectively led without such a leader? Lovett, as we have shown, condemned what he called 'leadership'. This could perhaps usefully be dispensed with for a small study and pressure group such as the London Working Men's Association. But the Chartist movement, which grew out of the work of the association, could not have been conducted upon such terms. As soon as the Charter was launched as a popular document a demagogue leader was needed. Lovett could not play the part: O'Connor was excellently equipped to do so.

Yet Lovett, Place and others at the time, followed by many historians since, have said that O'Connor's noisy demagoguery, far from making the movement, deprived it of all chance of success. The assumption is that parliament and government might have conceded the Charter to a quiet rational movement. In fact, this would not have happened. O'Connor's noisy methods may have provided parliament with one excuse for refusing the Charter; but in any case parliament regarded Chartist principles as quite impracticable, not worth serious consideration. The people lacked education; democracy would lead to anarchy and to confiscation of property. This was the theme, for example, of Macaulay's speech against the National Petition in 1842:

---

3. Harriet Martineau, *History of the Thirty Years' Peace* (1877 ed.), III, 489.

I believe that universal suffrage would be fatal to all purposes for which Government exists, and for which aristocracies and all other things exist, and that it is utterly incompatible with the very existence of civilisation. I conceive that civilisation rests upon the security of property . . . I will assert that while property is insecure, it is not in the power of the finest soil, or of the moral or intellectual constitution of any country, to prevent the country sinking into barbarism.

Macaulay's argument was generally accepted as sufficient answer to Lovett as well as to O'Connor.

In creating the Chartist movement as a popular agitation, O'Connor contributed little original thought to Chartist philosophy, although he often liked to pose as a theorist. This lack of intellectual originality has irritated some academic historians. They note that O'Connor took over the Charter intact from Lovett and Attwood. That even his Land Plan was derivative. But do we expect popular leaders to be original thinkers? Ernest Bevin, a modern popular leader, also used to appropriate the ideas of others and to repeat them as his own, 'often to the original source, with considerable self-congratulation and no acknowledgment'.[4] What may be conceded is that O'Connor could not judge very clearly even the ideas of others. The land dream was fundamentally unsound; yet he enthusiastically took it up and used his influence to induce thousands of working men to waste their savings. But Feargus O'Connor was not the first, nor the last, politician to advocate foolish policies.

Another charge against O'Connor has been that his language was exaggerated, that he threatened violence, violence which he did not even intend to employ. Three lines of defence are open here. Firstly, all popular movements require loud language to keep them going. Richard Cobden, who has gone down in history as a model politician, was almost as guilty as Feargus O'Connor of using threatening language during the 1840s. After one particularly violent attack upon Peel in 1845 Cobden had to excuse himself to his friends:[5]

You must not judge me by what I say at these tumultuous

---

4. A. Bullock, *Life and Times of Ernest Bevin*, I (1960), 369.
5. Morley, *Cobden*, 207-8.

public meetings. I constantly regret the necessity of violating good taste and kind feeling in my public harangues . . . I defy anybody to keep the ear of the public for seven years upon one question, without studying to amuse as well as instruct. People do not attend public meetings to be taught, but to be excited, flattered, and pleased . . . I have been obliged to amuse them, not by standing on my head or eating fire, but by kindred feats of jugglery, such as appeals to their self-esteem, their combativeness, or their humour.

Secondly in considering O'Connor's threatening language, we must not forget the terrible conditions of the time. Historians can talk easily about the 'Industrial Revolution', 'distress', the 'Irish problem' and other abstractions (this biography has done the same), but to contemporaries these were not abstractions but dark realities. They meant overwork or unemployment, bad food, bad housing, bad health—a short life and a miserable one. A visitor described the mood in Stockport in 1842 : 'words of hope are received with a shake of the head and a melancholy smile. "All that remains for me is to lay down and die" was the expression of a fine though faded young woman, when I expressed a hope that times would mend.'[6] Such an atmosphere often aroused desperate feelings in the audiences which O'Connor addressed. His emotional Irish temperament quickly responded to this mood of desperation. He sometimes used strong language because under the spur of deep distress his audiences wanted to hear him use it. Herbert Morrison has written of a similar reaction between speaker and audience in the case of Aneurin Bevan, an excitable Celt like O'Connor :[7]

At a political meeting he lives as part of his audience. He is partly its master and partly its creature. When he is speaking to an audience which is almost entirely on his side, and there is applause for something he says, he is sometimes tempted into saying something still more to his audience's liking in order to transform the applause into an ovation.

---

6. W. C. Taylor, *Tour in the Manufacturing Districts of Lancashire* (2nd ed., 1842), 186; J. G. Kohl, *Ireland, Scotland, and England* (1844), pt. 3, 123-24.
7. *Sunday Times,* April 3, 1960; Lord Morrison of Lambeth, *Herbert Morrison* (1960), 264.

O'Connor's feeling for popular suffering was certainly sincere. He felt deeply for the people and the people knew it. There was a ribald sincerity, a frantic courage in the man', admitted Charles Kingsley of him in *Alton Locke,* under the pseudonym of 'O'Flynn'. 'He always spoke the truth when it suited him, and very often when it did not. He did see, which is more than all do, that oppression is oppression, and humbug, humbug.'[8]

Finally in judging O'Connor's strong language as leader of the Chartists, we have to remember that up to a point at least it was deliberate bluff. O'Connor knew, as Lovett did not, that parliament and government would never concede the Charter to a quiet movement. He hoped to frighten them into concession. Three times, in 1838-39, in 1842 and in 1848, he tried the same line. It failed completely. Individuals were sometimes intimidated by O'Connor's tone, but government and parliament were always rightly confident that they could put down any outbreak if O'Connor should ever actually attempt one.[9]

Yet the attempt to stampede the authorities was worth making. Parliament and government had certainly been intimidated by threatening agitation during the Reform Bill crisis of 1831-32. The difference of course was that then the threats had come from the middle-classes with economic power behind them. They could threaten successfully : the working-classes could not. The failure of O'Connor's bluff proved this. In contemporary, social, economic and political circumstances the people could not achieve reform without the middle-classes beside them and without the final assistance of an enlightened parliamentarian, such as Peel. We have seen how O'Connor slowly learnt all this from his own failures. In his last years, although personally discredited, he persisted in pointing out the right road for working-class agitation in the future. With surprising self-abnegation he consistently placed Cobden and Peel before himself. He ignored the amused contempt with which they reacted to his praise in parliament. 'I am satisfied', he concluded in 1849, 'to leave the direction of the mind

---

8. C. Kingsley, *Alton Locke* (1881 ed.), II, 57.

9. See F. C. Mather, 'The Government and the Chartists' in Briggs (ed.), *Chartist Studies;* and *Public Order in the Age of the Chartists,* 39-45.

I have created and organised, to the discretion of those who possess more parliamentary influence than I do.'[10]

During the 1850s the working-classes were not much interested in agitating for parliamentary reform. Trade was mainly prosperous and working-class conditions were much improved compared with the previous decade. Ineffectual attempts were made throughout the '50s to keep up popular agitation. Harney tried unsuccessfully to regain popular support for the Chartist movement by transforming it into a proletarian socialist agitation. His socialism had led to a breach between him and O'Connor in 1850. Ernest Jones led the Chartist rump to the end of the '50s. By this date, like O'Connor and to the disgust of Marx and Engels, even Jones had come to see the need for some middle-class support for the working-class movement. Engels complained to Marx that 'the English proletariat is becoming more and more bourgeois . . . this most bourgeois of all nations is apparently aiming ultimately at the possession of a bourgeois aristocracy and a bourgeois proletariat *as well as* a bourgeoisie.'[11]

In the early 1860s under the stimulus of the American Civil War and of the visit of Garibaldi to England popular interest in parliamentary reform revived. A Reform League was set up which was in some respects in direct line with Chartism (many former Chartists were members). A Reform Union was founded which likewise had some connections with the Anti-Corn Law League. Some friction occurred between the two bodies but much less than between their predecessors of the 1840s. John Bright, who emphasised the need for 'a combined and friendly movement' and who was respected by members of both organisations, was able to draw the agitation in the country round himself. At Westminster, Gladstone, Peel's heir among parliamentarians, became a convert to extensive franchise reform. Finally, in 1867 the Second Reform Act was passed. Thus only twelve years after O'Connor's death many former Chartists were given the vote, in response to an agitation which had developed very much along the lines which in his last years he had recommended.

Thus out of failure came ultimate success for the working-class movement which O'Connor had led. And yet was O'Connor's

10. *Northern Star,* Aug. 18, 1849.
11. Schoyen, *Chartist Challenge,* 180-85, 195-97, 232; J. Saville (ed.), *Ernest Jones: Chartist* (1952), 62-63, 241-42.

work all failure even in his own day? We have shown that his most devoted followers were handloom weavers, framework knitters and others, victims of industrial transition, whose economic position was hopeless. During the Chartist years O'Connor's skilful demagoguery gave them hope. It was false hope, false like the Land Plan; but O'Connor did an important, if unconscious, service in helping to tide these obsolescent workmen over their protracted agony. By 1850 their problems were beginning to solve themselves. Their trades were being finally and mercifully extinguished by the complete introduction of machinery.

In only one respect did Feargus O'Connor almost completely fail, both in his own day and for the future. He was never able to create a real Anglo-Irish working-class alliance. Throughout the nineteenth and early twentieth centuries the popular movements of the two countries never became closely linked. Both would have been stronger and both might have been successful sooner if they had come together as Feargus O'Connor, who was both an Irishman and a Chartist, had so earnestly desired.

BIBLIOGRAPHY

Detailed bibliographies of the Chartist movement have been published in M. Hovell, *The Chartist Movement* (2nd ed., latest impr., 1959), G. D. H. Cole, *Chartist Portraits* (1941), and A. R. Schoyen, *The Chartist Challenge* (1958). We have not duplicated these lists here. Instead we give only those sources which have been found most useful in treating Chartism from O'Connor's point of view. This conveniently shortens our bibliography, although we include in it some Irish sources not previously used by historians of Chartism.

I. *Works by Feargus O'Connor* (O'Connor reprinted many of his open letters first published in the *Northern Star;* only the more important are noted here).

A State of Ireland, the Rise and Progress of the Present Disaffection (2nd ed., 1822).
A Letter from Feargus O'Connor, Esq., Barrister-at-Law, to His Excellency the Marquis of Anglesea (1832).
A Series of Letters from Feargus O'Connor, Esq., Barrister-at-Law, to Daniel O'Connell (1836).
The Remedy for National Poverty and Impending National Ruin: or the only Safe Way of Repealing the Corn Laws (1841).
Trial of Feargus O'Connor and Fifty-Eight Others at Lancaster (1843), with a commentary by F. O'Connor.
O'Connor, A. *State of Ireland* (1843 ed., intro, by F. O'Connor).
A Practical Work on the Management of Small Farms (1843).
Reply to Mr. John Watkins's Charges [1843].
Reply to Mr. Hill's 'Scabbard' [1843].
Reply of Feargus O'Connor, Esq. M.P., to the Charges against his Land and Labour Scheme (1847).

II. *Mss. Sources.*
Conner Papers (Manch House, Ballineen, Co. Cork).
Records of the King's Inns, Dublin.
Two letters from F. O'Connor to Serjeant Talfourd, M.P. (Castle Museum, York).
W. J. O'Neill Daunt, Journals and Letters (National Library of Ireland, Dublin).
Additional Mss. [Place] and Place Collection (British Museum).

Home Office Papers, 1836-48 (Public Record Office).
Lovett Collection (Birmingham Public Library).
Hovell Papers (Manchester University Library).

III. *Newspapers and Periodicals.*
Annual Register.
Anti-Bread-Tax Circular.
Bronterre's National Reformer.
The Charter.
Cleave's Weekly Police Gazette.
The Constitution; or Cork Advertiser.
Cork Evening Herald.
Cork Mercantile Chronicle.
Cork Southern Reporter.
Dublin Evening Post.
Edinburgh Review.
Evening Star.
Fraser's Magazine.
Gentleman's Magazine.
The Labourer.
The League.
Leeds Intelligencer.
Leeds Mercury.
Leeds Times.
Manchester Examiner.
Manchester Guardian.
Manchester Times.
Manchester & Salford Advertiser.
National Instructor.
Northern Star.
Notes to the People.
Nottingham Journal.
Nottingham Mercury.
Nottingham Review.
Nottingham Telegraph.
People's Paper.
People's Press and Cork Weekly Gazette.
Political Register.
Poor Man's Guardian.
Reynolds's Weekly Political Instructor.
The Times.

IV. *Printed Sources.*
Adams, W. E. *Memoirs of a Social Atom* (1903).
Armytage, W. H. G. 'The Chartist Land Colonies 1846-48', *Agricultural History*, vol. 32 (1958).
Aspinall, A. (ed.) *Three Early Nineteenth Century Diaries* (1952).
Baxter, G. R. W. *Book of the Bastilles* (1841).

Beer, M. *A History of British Socialism* (1919-21).

Briggs, A. (ed.) *Chartist Studies* (1959).

—— 'Chartism Reconsidered', in *Historical Studies,* Papers read before the Third Conference of Irish Historians (ed. M. Roberts, 1959).

Burke, Sir J. B. *A Second Series of Vicissitudes of Families* (1860).

Burtchaell, C. G. D. & Sadleir, T.U. (eds.) *Alumni Dublinenses* (new ed., 1935).

Chambers's Biographical Dictionary (1956 ed.).

Journal of Henry Cockburn (1874).

Cole, G. D. H. *Life of William Cobbett* (3rd ed., 1947).

—— *Chartist Portraits* (1941).

The Life of Thomas Cooper, by Himself (2nd ed., 1872).

Dalby, G. R. 'The Chartist Movement in Halifax and District', *Trans. Halifax Antiquarian Society,* 1956.

Daunt, W. J. O'Neill. *Ireland and her Agitators* (1845).

—— *Personal Recollections of the late Daniel O'Connell* (1848).

—— 'Feargus O'Connor. A Memoir'. *Young Ireland,* V (1879).

—— *Eighty-Five Years of Irish History 1800-1885* (1886).

—— *A Life Spent for Ireland* (1896).

Dictionary of National Biography.

Duffy, Sir C. G. *Four Years of Irish History* (1883).

Duncombe, T. H. *Life and Correspondence of Thomas Slingsby Duncombe* (1868).

Edwards, R. O. & Williams T. O. (eds.) *The Great Famine* (1956).

Elt, C. H. & Allen, S. *Complete Suffrage and Feargus O'Connor* (1844).

Engels, F. *The Condition of the Working Class in England* (trans. W. O. Henderson & W. H. Chaloner, 1958).

Fagan, W. *Life and Times of Daniel O'Connell* (1848).

Fairlie, H. 'Oratory in Political Life', *History Today,* X (1960).

Fitzpatrick, W. J. (ed.) *Correspondence of Daniel O'Connell* (1888).

Foster, J. *Register of Admissions to Gray's Inn, 1521-1889* (p.p., 1889).

Frost, T. *Forty Years' Recollections* (1880).

Gammage, R. G. *History of the Chartist Movement* (2nd ed., 1894).

Glasgow, E. L. H. 'The Establishment of the *Northern Star* Newspaper', *History,* XXXIX (1954).

[Grant, J.] *Random Recollections of the House of Commons* (3rd ed., 1836).

Gillespie, Frances E. *Labour and Politics in England 1850-1867* (1927).

Hill, W. *A Scabbard for Feargus O'Connor's Sword* (1843).

Holyoake, G. J. *Life of Joseph Rayner Stephens* (1881).

Hovell, M. *The Chartist Movement* (2nd ed., 1959 impr.).

Inglis, B. *Freedom of the Press in Ireland 1784-1841* (1954).

Jackson, J. *The Demagogue done up: an Exposure of the Extreme Inconsistencies of Mr. Feargus O'Connor* (1844).

Jennings, L.J. (ed.) *Correspondence and Diaries of . . . John Wilson Croker* (2nd ed., 1885).

Jephson, H. *The Platform* (1892).

Jones, E. *Vindication of the Dead* : *O'Connor versus Mursell* (1859).

Jones, W. *Funeral Oration on Feargus O'Connor* (1855).

Journals of the House of Commons.

Kingsley, C. *Alton Locke* (1881 ed.).

Knapp, J. W. & Ombler, E. *Cases of Controverted Elections in the Twelfth Parliament of the United Kingdom* (1837).

Kohl, J. G. *Ireland, Scotland, and England* (1844).

Lampson, G. L. *A Consideration of the State of Ireland in the Nineteenth Century* (1907).

Leader, R. E. *Life and Letters of John Arthur Roebuck* (1897).

Lewis, S. *A Topographical Dictionary of Ireland* (2nd ed., 1847).

Life and Struggles of William Lovett (1920 ed.).

McCarthy, J. *Reminiscences* (1899).

Maccoby, S. *English Radicalism 1832-1852* (1935).

McCord, N. *The Anti-Corn Law League* (1958).

McDowell, R. B. *Public Opinion and Government Policy in Ireland, 1801-1846* (1952).

Madden, R. R. *The United Irishmen*, second series, second ed. (1857-60).

—— *History of Irish Periodical Literature* (1867).

Maddon, D. O. *Ireland and its Rulers since 1829* (1843-45).

Mather, F. C. *Public Order in the Age of the Chartists* (1959).

Matthews, R. C. O. *A Study in Trade-Cycle History. Economic Fluctuations in Great Britain 1833-1842* (1954).

Morley, J. *Life of Richard Cobden* (1903 ed.).

Musson, A. E. *The Typographical Association* (1954).

Napier, Sir W. F. P. *Life and Opinions of Sir Charles James Napier* (1857).

Oastler, R. *West Riding Nomination Riot: A Letter to Viscount Morpeth* (1837).

O'Connell, J. *Recollections and Experiences during a Parliamentary Career* (1849).

Parliamentary Accounts & Papers.

Parliamentary Debates.

Patterson, M. W. *Sir Francis Burdett and his Times* (1931).

Philp, R. K. *Vindication of his Political Conduct and an Exposition of the Misrepresentations of the Northern Star* (1842).

Personal Remembrances of Sir Frederick Pollock (1887).

Prentice, A. *History of the Anti-Corn Law League* (1853).

Robinson, W. B. *A Letter addressed to the Trades . . . on the National Land Company, and the National Land and Labour Bank* (1847).

Rose, A. G. 'The Plug Riots of 1842 in Lancashire and Cheshire', *Trans. Lancashire & Cheshire Antiquarian Society*, LXVII (1957).

Rothstein, T. *From Chartism to Labourism* (1929).

Saville, J. (ed.) *Ernest Jones: Chartist* (1952).

Schoyen, A. R. *The Chartist Challenge* (1958).
Stanley, A. P. *Life of Thomas Arnold* (1904 ed.).
Taylor, W. C. *Tour in the Manufacturing Districts of Lancashire* (2nd ed., 1842).
Tinsley, W. *Random Recollections of an Old Publisher* (1900).
Letters of Queen Victoria (1908).
Ward, J. T. 'Revolutionary Tory: the Life of Joseph Rayner Stephens of Ashton-under-Lyne (1805-1879)', *Trans, Lancashire & Cheshire Antiquarian Society*, LXVIII (1958).
Watkins, J. *Impeachment of Feargus O'Connor* (1843).
Williams, D. *John Frost* (1939).
Wilson, B. *Struggles of an Old Chartist* (1887).
Wood, A. C. 'Nottingham 1835-1865', *Trans. Thoroton Society*, LIX (1955).
Wright, L. C. *Scottish Chartism* (1953).

V. *Theses.*

O'Higgins, Rachel, *Ireland and Chartism*. A study of the Influence of Irishmen and the Irish Question on the Chartist Movement (Ph. D. thesis, Trinity College, Dublin, 1959).
Jones, R. *The Social and Political Importance of the Irish in Manchester 1838-48* (B. A. thesis, Leeds University, 1961).

INDEX

Acland, J., on Plug Strikes, 103-4.
Allsop, T., advice to O'Connor, 132-33, 134.
Alton Locke, quoted on O'Connor, 149.
Anti-Corn Law League, conflict with Chartists, 92-94, 118-20 ; formed, 68 ; and Plug Strikes, 103-4.
Arnold, T., on problems of industrial society, 43.
Attwood, T., attitude of towards National Convention, 82; leader of B.P.U., 68; O'Connor promises to follow, 69; O'Connor overshadows, 80.

Barnsley, centre of O'Connor cult, 76-78 ; decline of O'Connor's influence at, 137-38 ; Radical newspaper projected at, 57.
Barry, G. S., 30, 37.
Bernard, James, 51.
    Lord, 30, 37.
Bevan, A., compared with O'Connor, 148.
Bevin, E., compared with O'Connor, 147.
Birmingham, Bull Ring outrage at, 84-85 ; Chartist meeting at (Aug. 6, 1838), 69-70, 75 ; Complete Suffrage conference at, 101, 106 ; removal of National Convention to, 83-84 ; social structure of and Chartism, 42.
Birmingham Political Union, address to English and Irish people, 76 ; delegates' withdrawal from National Convention, 82 ; and National Convention, 68 ; and National Petition, 68 ; O'Connor's differences with, 78, 80. (See also under *Attwood, T.*).
Bradford, support for *Northern Star* at, 58-59.
Bradshaw, J., O'Connor prosecutes, 115-16.
Bright, J., and ' Little Charter ', 136 ; and Plug Strikes, 103 ; and Second Reform Act, 150.
Burdett, Sir F., attracted to Feargus O'Connor, 19 ; friend of Roger O'Connor, 13, 19.
Burnley, 102.

Carrington, 98.
Central National Association, 51.
Charter, the People's, ignored by O'Connor, 62, 68 ; O'Connor supports, 69 ; its points anticipated, 46, 66 ; published, 62, 66, 68.
Charter, The, 63.
Charterville, 114, 116.
Cheshire, support for 1842 petition in, 99.
Clontarf, repeal meeting at abandoned, 123.

Cobbett, John Morgan, 45.
    William, 15, 32 ; death of, 44-45 ; O'Connor aims to succeed, 45, 51, 60, 62, 108.
Cobden, R., Cobden's use of strong language, 147-48 ; leads Anti-Corn Law League, 43, 118-119 ; Northampton meeting with O'Connor, 119-20 ; O'Connor's changed attitude towards, 120, 136, 149 ; opposes Chartism, 42, 119 ; and Plug Strikes, 103.
Complete Suffrage movement, begins, 101 ; O'Brien supports, 95, 101 ; O'Connor destroys, 106 (See also under *Sturge, J.*).
Conner, Cornelius, 9-10.
    Daniel (i), 10 ; Daniel (ii), 10 ; Daniel (iii), 11.
    Roger, 10.
    Robert, career of, 11, 12 ; leaves Fort Robert to Feargus O'Connor, 20.
    William, 10.
Connerville, built, 10 ; probable birthplace of Feargus O'Connor, 16.
Cooper, T., attacks O'Connor, 145 ; impressed by O'Connor, 17, 95-96 ; at Nottingham bye-election, 102 ; on influence of patriotic reputation of O'Connor family, 12.
Cork, Co., state of in 1820s, 24-25.
Cork Southern Reporter, on O'Connor, 27, 31, 37 ; O'Connor attempts to buy, 126.
Corn Laws, see under *Anti-Corn Law League*.

Daunt, W. J. O'Neill, on O'Connor, 15, 20, 29, 108, 144.
Democrat, The, projected newspaper, 64.
Doheny, M., 129 ; on O'Connor, 130.
Doherty, J., 67.
Dorchester labourers, O'Connor supports, 44, 46.
Douglas, R. K., 68.
Duffy, C. G., 123, 138.
Duncombe, T. S., O'Connor offers to follow, 125 ; presents 1842 petition, 99.
Dungarvan, O'Connor and bye-election at, 35-36.

East London Democratic Association, O'Connor supports, 50-51, 74-75, 79.
Edinburgh Review, on Land Plan, 114-15.
Engels, F., disappointment with Chartists, 150 ; praises O'Connor, 127-28.
Enniskeen, O'Connor's meetings at, 27, 88.

DATE DUE